FROM 6 TO 7 FIGURES

DOWNLOAD THE AUDIOBOOK (FREE)!

Read This First

To say thanks for reading this book, I would like to give you the audio-book version 100% FREE!

I know this book can and *will* change your life if you read it…and you're more likely to do so if you have the audiobook.

I narrated it myself and go into a bit more detail for examples, so I highly recommend both.

Instead of paying $15-20 for the audiobook, it's my gift to you for free…

>> 2X.co/audio <<

PRAISE FOR
FROM 6 TO 7 FIGURES

"This is the playbook that entrepreneurs NEED. Step by step, Austin shares what matters most to get free and grow."

Dan Martell
B2B SaaS Growth Coach & Investor

"This book will save you years and get you on the fast-track to create the financial freedom and cash flow you desire."

John Lee Dumas
Host of the award winning podcast, *Entrepreneurs On Fire*

"Most small business owners are slaves to their businesses, Austin shows you how to build a business that serves you and not the other way around."

Dr. Saman Bakhtiar
CEO, *The Camp Transformation Centers International*

"This book is designed to help you get off of the 6-figure hamster-wheel. There isn't anyone better than Austin to help make that happen."

Jack Haldrup
Founder & CEO, *Dr. Squatch Soap Co.*

"From 6 to 7 Figures goes into topics that aren't talked about nearly enough—systems, operations, team, hiring, finances, execution. This is the stuff that matters, not just some new marketing strategy. Entrepreneurs, you can't afford not to read this."

Chandler Bolt
Founder & CEO, *Self Publishing School*

"I've helped build over 100 businesses scale past 7 figures and the #1 thing I've discovered? If you don't have what Austin talks about in this book, you're going to slow down your momentum, profitability (and happiness)."

Scott Oldford
Entrepreneur Mentor, Advisor & Investor

"Austin has mastered turning your business into a machine. This practical guide is timeless and recession-proof knowledge that will serve entrepreneurs for their whole career."

Dan Schwartz
CEO, *InvestorFuse*

"If you're wanting focused accelerated growth, then apply what you see in this outstanding business reference. Austin has put together the most practical and action-oriented strategies that will extract maximum value, immediate revenue impact, and develop long-term compounding revenue opportunities for your business."

John Logar
Founder, *Consulting Unleashed*

FROM 6 TO 7 FIGURES

UPDATED & EXPANDED

The Proven Playbook
To Get More Traction,
Free Up 20 Hours Per Week,
And Scale Past $1M
In Revenue!

AUSTIN NETZLEY

FOUNDER OF 2X

From 6 To 7 Figures
The Proven Playbook To Get More Traction, Free Up 20 Hours Per Week, And Scale Past $1M In Revenue!

Printed in the United States of America

ISBN-13: 978-0-578-28798-0

Interior Design by FormattedBooks.com

DEDICATION

To my nephews,

I don't care if either of you ever become an entrepreneur, but you help me be a better one by reminding me what matters most.

TABLE OF CONTENTS

INTRODUCTION

I knew I should have been at seven figures by now.

I had the talent, work ethic, and potential. Yet here I was—stuck at six figures in revenue. I felt like I hit a wall.

More hours? More grit? Trying more tactics and a bigger team? None of it worked.

The excitement and allure that got me into entrepreneurship were gone. The freedom, the growth, the impact and limitless upside—it was all a *lie*. I was exhausted and burnt out.

I realized I didn't actually have a business. I had a self-employed J.O.B. that required more work and paid less money than my corporate career. I was on the six-figure hamster wheel, going nowhere fast.

Then, it hit me…

What gets you to six figures in revenue is NOT what will get you to multiple millions.

WHAT GOT YOU HERE

XVIII | FROM 6 TO 7 FIGURES

The Path To 7 Figures

Congrats, you've made it to six figures as an entrepreneur! That felt like an accomplishment at the beginning, but you know you're destined for so much more.

You want to get past that magic $1 million revenue mark once and for all, but getting there hasn't been as easy as you thought it would be. You've put in the hours, blood, sweat, and tears, and gave your business your all…

Only to be stuck in a pretty similar position with the same problems and headaches (no consistent leads, cash flow concerns, team stresses, etc.) to where you were a year ago.

Why is that?

It's because **what got you to six figures—the thinking, key actions, strategies and habits—will *not* be what gets you to seven figures**.

In fact, most of what you have done (and are still doing now) are the *exact* things holding you back from the next level. The constant hustle and grind. The do-it-all-yourself mentality. Being pulled in so many different directions. Making short-term decisions to survive. All of that has to come to an end.

There is a much simpler and better path to scale, and that's what I'm about to show you in this book. After now working with hundreds of entrepreneurs and businesses directly, I've learned a very important lesson:

There is a formula for business success. And there is a very important *order* to things to get the most traction possible.

The ones that succeed do well in a few critical areas. And the ones that grow the *fastest* while NOT working crazy hours also approach their growth by following this very strategic *order*. So, I'm going to walk you through step-by-step how to approach your growth as you head towards multiple millions the *right* way.

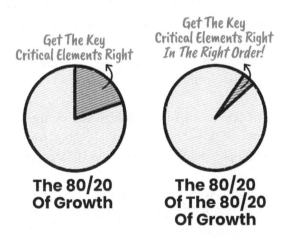

The 80/20 Of Growth

The 80/20 Of The 80/20 Of Growth

There are seven steps, each one sequentially building on top of each other to help you take back control of your time and business…and get you on the fast-track to a multimillion-dollar business that works *for you*—not the other way around.

And trust me, this stuff flat-out works.

I've now built three seven-figure companies in a few short years and have helped countless entrepreneurs across the globe do the same with this proven playbook.

My company, 2X, works with six- and seven-figure entrepreneurs all over the globe. In our first three years of business, we've used these proven systems and strategies I'm about to share with you to help generate over $255 million in client revenue while *in* our 2X programs; this doesn't count what happens after they finish our programs!

This is the exact step-by-step methodology that we used to help John Murphy go from $67k per month and 110 hour work weeks (seriously!)... to $503k per month while working 10 hours per week. In six months time!

And how Ryan Rockwell 10X'ed his business from $31k per month to over $307k per month, while also being able to take a month completely off to travel to South Africa.

And how we helped Erin Green go from zero weekends off in twenty years as an entrepreneur…to taking every weekend and two entire weeks off all in her first 60 days after implementing these strategies.

By taking these steps, you'll transform your business from *owning you* to you being in complete control.

It's about consistent, predictable growth.

Just follow the process, step by step.

The Numbers To $1+ Million

The fact of the matter is that most businesses fail. Michael Gerber, author of the great book *The E-Myth Revisited* famously shared that 80% of businesses fail in the first five years. And of those that survive, 80% will fail in the next five years!

Even more, of those that do survive, even with all of the effort put into their business, only 40% are profitable, 30% break even, and 30% continually *lose* money.[1] That's depressing!

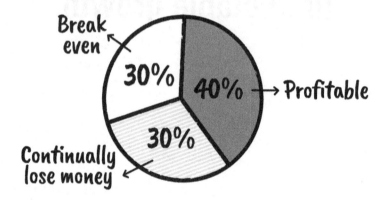

But you're different.

If you're reading this book, business failure isn't really as much a concern as not achieving near your potential—which can feel even worse. And what you know is possible is having a seven-figure business and the lifestyle you started as an entrepreneur to achieve.

The bad thing is, the stats of having a million-dollar business are equally disappointing. Only 4% achieve seven figures or more.[2]

[1] Wallace, David. "Infographic: The Most Tried And Failed Small Businesses." *Small Business Trends*, 15 March 2013, https://smallbiztrends.com/2013/03/infographic-failed-small-businesses.html

[2] Harnish, Verne. *Scaling Up*. Gazelles, Inc., 2014

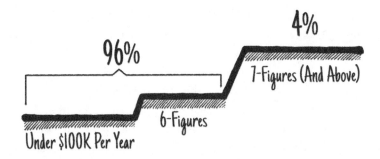

96%

4%

Under $100K Per Year

6-Figures

7-Figures (And Above)

Put another way, **96% of businesses *fail* to get to $1 million!** My company is on a mission to change that head-on by sharing the proven playbook.

The cool thing is, I have yet to meet many six-figure entrepreneurs who aren't just a few simple (but vital) tweaks away from getting to that magic million-dollar mark. I'm guessing it's the same for you.

To reach the 4% club, we need to get you to a minimum of $83,333 per month…and have it be consistent and controlled. That's what I'll guide you on.

$1 Million	Per Year
$83,333	Per Month
$19,178	Per Week

We'll take it step by step to make sure you not only reach the growth you want, but that you are set up so that your new highs become your new lows and you continue to level up in the future. **Consistency and control are key.**

The challenge with so many businesses failing and not growing—and your business not growing in the way you want—is that it's not your fault! You have been given the wrong advice based around short-term tactics and hacks by the countless "gurus" out there fighting for your attention. They have to make their offers exciting and feel *new* when, in reality, the stuff that works now are the same principles that mattered 100 years ago.

So, in this book, we're going to skip the short-term hacks. I'm going to skip telling you what you want to hear. We are going to go back to the principles; the *essential* elements that you must get right. We are not going to talk about Facebook Ads hacks, how to get more social media followers, or anything tactical.

We are, however, going to talk about:

- Making sure you have a seven-figure strategy and business model set up to scale
- Getting you free from the weeds and to stop being *owned* by your business
- How to build a world-class team that produces results (without you!)
- And turning your business into a consistent, predictable, cash-producing *machine* to set you up for many years to come

My goal is to forever change the way you see—and operate—your business. The end result is not only more revenue growth than ever, but more importantly, more freedom, fun, consistency, profit, impact, and opportunities.

It's time to unleash your full potential and help you achieve that vision for why you started in business to begin with. This book will be your guide.

The Free 7-Figure Toolkit

Now, this is important to note: To achieve big success, it's not about ideas or information. **It's about implementation and execution.**

To help, I'll be sharing a lot of proven strategies and systems that we use ourselves and with our private clients at 2X. So, I put together a complete toolkit of resources I share in the book including:

- Specific templates
- Example spreadsheets
- Custom PDF worksheets to fill in
- Deep-dive training videos
- And more

All included for FREE to help put these strategies into action. You can access all of these tools directly here:

>> 2X.co/toolkit <<

You'll see me reference this link numerous times throughout, so take advantage and set yourself up for years to come.

And as you go through this, I'm here to help you. Shoot me an email anytime directly at <u>austin@2x.co</u> and I'll support you in getting clear and building momentum. Let's get you to seven figures fast!

THE MILLION-DOLLAR MINDSET & VISION

The Iceberg Under It All

There is a proven formula to successfully scale a six- or seven-figure online or service-based business. We have worked to master this methodology, and call it the 2X Formula. It's one of the key frameworks we use to help entrepreneurs grow fast.

There are nine elements involved, and the key element that encompasses it all is your **mindset**. This is where it all starts and ends.

Without the right mindset, nothing else matters. You can have the best model, an amazing product/service, and be in the right market, but will still fail if you don't get your mind right.

Much like an iceberg, your mindset goes much deeper than you'd expect. It impacts your vision, decision-making, risk-taking, ability to let go, leadership, action-taking, consistency, attitude toward failures and challenges, and more. Long story short, it's the foundation for everything that few entrepreneurs really work on.

But it's clear: look at the most successful entrepreneurs around, and you'll see they have a different mentality. That's no coincidence. Get this right and entrepreneurship is truly limitless in what you can achieve.

So, we'll start here with what you need to know and adjust to create your million-dollar CEO mindset and vision…

The Hardest Part

Business is easy.

It's my job to convince you of this by showing you what matters and what doesn't. But some aspects of business *are* difficult. Potentially the hardest part of all for entrepreneurs is this:

Figuring out what you really want!

Most entrepreneurs have no idea what they truly want. Caught up in the day-to-day blur, it's easy to forget why you became an entrepreneur to begin with. But what are you working so hard for? What is the end goal?

Before we go any further, *stop* and think.

> What do you really want from your business? What is your ideal situation? How many hours do you want to work? Where are you headed? What is true success for you? And what does your ideal life and lifestyle look like?

You don't get in the car until you know where you're going...

and you shouldn't be working so hard driving your business without a clear and exciting destination in mind either!

Because your business is a tool. **It's a *tool* to create your dream life.** It's the *vehicle* to help you create the life and lifestyle you know is possible. It's not your job. It's not who you are. It's a separate entity that should be used to create that ideal situation for you and your family.

Before we talk about anything related to your business, we have to get clear on your personal vision first. The clearer and more compelling this is, the faster you can go.

Clarity creates speed.

All future business decisions only make sense once we know this. And then from there, it's time to create your business vision too (which will be aligned but not about you).

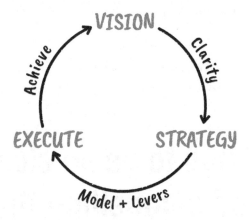

This business vision will then be your big-picture guide for your team and company. That's your north star.

To define this, imagine yourself three years out. Put yourself in that time. Imagine your business, your life, the feelings and emotions, the accomplishments, your team, the environment around you, your family. Create a full detailed picture in your mind and then write it down.

What does this look like? What does it *feel* like? What milestones and results are you going to achieve a couple years out as a company?

This vision you're creating is the destination. Everything we do— from strategy to your team to your model and which marketing channels to focus on—will be designed to get you *there* to your personal and business vision as fast as possible.

We love the three-year time frame because it's far enough out for you to break from your current situation and design exactly what you want, but it's not so far out that your goals feel like fantasies. The challenge is taking the time to get clear on this. Most are 'too busy' to think about this critically, and as a result don't ever have that vision…And as a result, don't achieve the life, freedom, wealth and impact they work so hard for. So don't be that person. Stop and think first. This is the best thing you can do.

There's so much you *could* do and have; it's just up to you to decide. To have a vision that works, you have to get specific.

It has to be so clear and compelling that you and your team can see it and *feel* it.

This is what will get you fired up to keep pushing through the hard times, and has to keep you saying "no" to the many opportunities that try to pull you off your path. Plus, the bigger and more clear your vision, the smaller the day-to-day challenges are.

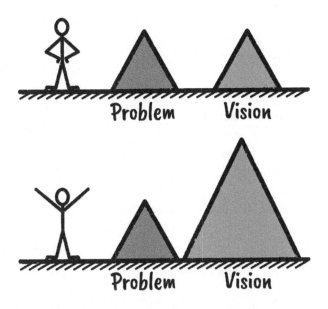

This is essential, as even though you're about to learn how to turn your business into a high-performing machine…it's *not* going to be all sunshine and rainbows.

There *will* be challenges.
There *will* be difficult conversations.
There *will* be some stressful situations.
There *will* be a few big decisions to make.
There *will* be times when you question, *is it all worth it?*

When you signed up for this entrepreneurship thing, you signed up for all of this (and more). But with a clear and compelling vision of your personal life and company, you'll see what is possible if you make it through. And using the principles in this book, you *will* make it through.

So I highly encourage you: Take some time, get outside or away from your normal workplace and environment, and craft a 3- to 10-page overview of exactly where you'll be three years from now. Define the future and create a document to share around. Cameron Herold's Vivid Vision process is invaluable here.

Here are a few signs that you have the right, clear, compelling vision:

> You can also see our example vision and template in your 7-Figure Toolkit at 2X.co/toolkit.

1. You can see it and FEEL your vision as if you're already there!

2. There is a bigger purpose or mission to it other than making money.

3. It makes you smile even simply thinking about it.

4. It's a bit scary and will stretch you; but you still believe to your core it can (and will) happen.

5. It helps you realize that 99% of the challenges you face are minuscule compared to where you're going. They're nothing but tests to make you stronger.

6. It helps you attract your dream team into your life in and out of business—clients, employees, spouse, friends, partners—that also have the same vision and values.

7. And it doesn't change much. Once you have the right complete vision, it feels so aligned that it can adapt and mold some, but it doesn't change every few months with another idea or direction.

As soon as you get there, you're off to the races. From here, it's a lot easier to make the necessary decisions to get there. This will be your north star. This is critical not only for you, but especially for your team. They'll be able to see what you see, keeping everyone moving toward the mission at hand.

From there, we'll reverse-engineer the fastest, most strategic path to make it a reality. But nothing matters until you have this.

6-Figure Hustler	7-Figure CEO
• General goals, often changing • No clearly defined business vision • Team isn't very clear on the company direction and overall mission	• You have a specific, compelling personal and business visions • Team is aligned and clear on the company vision and mission • Team (and CEO) uses the vision as the guide to help stay focused on what matters most

WHO You Have To Become

Now, thinking about your future and what you want to accomplish—the growth, the income, the impact...To make it a reality, *what has to happen?*

More importantly,

WHO do you have to become to make this vision a reality?

You've gotten to this point because of who you have been and who you are now. But to get your business to the next level, you have to first get your*self* to the next level. The fact is, your business will never far exceed where you're at as the leader.

And the cool thing is, you can design whoever you want. My favorite Tony Robbins lesson of all is him talking about the icon that we all know today. He said, *"Tony Robbins didn't exist. I created this mother******* standing here."*

Yes, he was born with some natural skills and talents. But much more than that, he *designed* who he needed to be. He crafted that person and worked at it daily. As soon as I learned this, I went on to design who I needed to be too.

I went from not having confidence to having more than almost anyone I know. I told myself every day I was a master of systems years before I was. I designed who I wanted (and *needed*) to be, and worked at it every day. Soon enough, I realized I became that person and started achieving the results and life I dreamed of. You can do the same. In fact, to get to the next level, you *need* to do the same.

So let's begin defining the next version of you using this simple exercise.

Start by making a line down a page like this graphic below. On the left side, list out the key traits and qualities of how you'd describe how you've been as CEO in the past. How would your team and others really describe you? List those out first.

**The Old You
(6-figures)**

**The New You
(7-figures)**

Then think about the qualities of who you need to be that will make you the CEO of a multimillion-dollar business.

What are your key traits and qualities?
How do you treat and protect your time?
What habits and principles do you live by?
What key shifts do you need to make?

And *how is this list different from who you've been in the past?*

Go deep on this. Write out the characteristics and changes needed. Then, start being that new CEO today! You don't have to wait. Even create an alter ego if you have to.

That's what worked for one of our 2X Accelerator clients, Ulyses Osuna of *Influencer Press*. On day one, we realized he had dreams like many entrepreneurs do—to finally run a million-dollar business. The problem is, his mentality was stuck in the low six figures, which was unsurprisingly where he had been for years.

To get to the next level, we needed the next version of him—so we started calling him 'U7' to remind him of the decisions that the *'seven-figure Ulyses'* would make.

U7 handled problems, challenges, and decisions differently. He protected his time, stopped making short-term reactive decisions, built a team for the long-term, and did what it took to make his compelling vision a reality. Now, he's transformed into an entirely new person, CEO, and business man living his dream life.

That's what you need to do too. Design who that next-level version of you needs to be to accomplish your big goals...**And start being that person today!**

It's time. As soon as you do, you'll officially be on the path to seven figures.

6-Figure Hustler	7-Figure CEO
Characteristics and Traits: Busy, Unable To Let Go, Weak Leadership, Afraid To Take Risk, Inconsistent, Distracted Easily, Focused On Tactics	Characteristics and Traits: Protects Time Like Gold, Strategic & Intentional, Confident, Clear, Consistent, Building A Machine, Playing The Long Game, Keeps Things Simple, Focused

CEO Problem-Solving Mentality

As you've discovered, the first major difference between struggling and elite entrepreneurs is with the mind.

When a new project, opportunity, or issue comes up, a six-figure CEO immediately thinks:

How am I going to get this done?
What do I need to do?
But what about {insert excuse/fear/tactical question}?

They immediately start thinking about *how* it's going to happen. They get excited by doing something 'new and shiny,' delaying what they know they *need* to do. They start asking tactical and technical questions about small details, and their minds start *adding on more and more stuff* to an increasingly overwhelming to-do list.

Sound familiar?

This is how I was for years, and part of the reason why I had so many six-figure businesses. But then I learned…a seven-figure CEO just *thinks* differently.

When a new project or opportunity comes up, **the seven-figure CEO thinks first about alignment with their future vision and whether or not it is essential**. The reality is, most things are busywork and not aligned or strategic to help you achieve your vision. So this is a huge first step.

Then, if it is aligned, they think two very important things:

1. *Who should own this project?*

2. *What systems are needed?*

This is completely different from how six-figure CEOs think.

"*Who* and *what* systems…not *how*."

You come up with a new project that has potential for a big ROI? Great. Instead of immediately taking it on and adding yet another thing to your plate, stop and think:

> *Who is going to own this project? And what systems do they need to make it an ongoing success?*

What happens if a fire comes up? Sure, it happens (hopefully less and less), but instead of hopping in and handling it yourself like normal, think:

> *Who is going to own this issue? And what systems do we need to have so this never comes up again?*

This simple mentality will keep you out of the weeds, empower your team, improve your operations, and ultimately allow you to grow your company better and faster than ever. It's a subtle difference that makes a massive impact.

Not everything can (or should!) come from you, so change your mentality, start doing less, and think like a seven-figure CEO.

Think: *Is it aligned?*
Is it essential?

And then…

Who *will own this?* **And what systems** *are needed?*

This simple yet game-changing mindset tweak will keep you flying high on the fast-path to millions.

6-Figure Hustler	7-Figure CEO
• "Do-It-All" mentality • Thinks HOW to do something and about the tactical details • Takes on responsibility for almost all problems and opportunities • Can't let go or delegate • Fixes problems at the surface level, putting out fires but not fixing the source	• Thinks *"Who & What Systems?"* not *"HOW?"* to do something • Fixes problems at the source, solving things for the long-term • Empowers team to execute and lead • Stays free from the weeds!

CEO Survival 101

Business is an intense sport, especially when you have big goals and want to grow fast. To not only survive, but thrive, there is one crucial skill you have to master. That skill is represented by this crazy story I once read about 'smokejumpers.'

These are highly trained, elite firefighters that parachute into active wild-fires to stop the spreading blaze. It's clearly one of the most dangerous jobs on the planet—firefighters risking their lives in the wild to save countless others.

The story goes that 15 of them were deep in a spreading fire trying to contain it when things suddenly changed. The winds shifted, and the fire started surrounding them. Being stuck in a canyon, there was only one way out...

Up the mountain.

Wearing the heavy gear and carrying tools needed to fight the fire, the smokejumpers faced a near-impossible task to survive.

Of the 15, only three survived.

In the aftermath analysis of the fire, the report found there was one key difference among the three survivors:

> All three *let go* of the weight holding them back. The other 12 who tragically died didn't get rid of the 100-plus pounds of gear until it was too late.

This story represents so much of what entrepreneurship is and what it takes. It's a climb up a mountain with a ton of things that can hold you back: your mindset, your beliefs, the economy, competition chasing you, coronavirus, and an endless list of other challenges.

In business, the ones who not only survive but thrive are the ones who *let go*.

This is not easy at first. You got to where you are by holding on so tight to driving results yourself. But I'm telling you, your business livelihood, and all the incredible success that is possible for you, depends on it.

Let go. Cut the weight holding you back. And step into the upgraded seven-figure version of yourself.

6-Figure Hustler	7-Figure CEO
• Afraid to let go • Thinks it's better/faster/cheaper to *"just do it myself"* and as a result keeps doing too much (staying on the hamster-wheel) • Doesn't trust in others or empower the team • Focused on short-term actions instead of long-term team development	• Knows that to get where they want to go they must *let go* • Cuts out the non-essential and is focused on the highest impact activities to drive results • Consistently thinks how to work "on" the business, not be stuck "in" it • Empowers the team to grow and develop

Chapter 1 Big Ideas

- Your business will never far exceed your mindset; to take your business to the next level, you must start here with the mind.
- The only way to achieve your vision is to first get hyper clear on what it is! Your vision drives every business decision. This is your north star.
  - o You need to craft a clear and compelling personal and business vision so that we can design the business and strategies to get you *there*, as doing all of the work doesn't matter if it doesn't help you achieve your goals.
  - o The challenge is, the hardest thing of all is to figure out what you *really* want. You must stop and think, getting out of the day-to-day grind to think and get clear. Again, this drives everything.
- The more clear you and your team are, the faster you can go. It's worth it to spend the extra time up front to get clear, focused and aligned!
- Once you're clear on your vision, the question to ask is WHO do you have to become to make that a reality? Define and detail this person, as well as what's been holding you back. And start to make the shift today!
- With any challenge or new project, start to think like a seven-figure CEO. Think *"who and what systems"*... not *"how"* you're going to do something. This will keep you free from the weeds and working "on" the business.
- To achieve your big goals, you have to learn to *let go*. You can't do it all yourself, and you shouldn't try! This is one of the make-or-break skills to develop as you scale to multiple millions.

CHAPTER 2

YOUR 7-FIGURE STRATEGY

Market Domination With Model ONE™

You now have a clear image of where you want to go and what you want to achieve. Now it's time to create the right strategy that helps you achieve your vision as quickly and easily as possible.

When thinking about strategy, most newbie and six-figure entrepreneurs think about tactics. They're looking for the latest marketing hack, advertising trick, a new fancy funnel or tool. They think these are the answers that will unlock growth. But if you've tried those things, you know that it's not the answer.

The true answer is with a killer strategy. This is the 80/20 of growth. At 2X, we define strategy as:

1. The **structure** for your business, and how it's set up to scale (your business model).

2. Your go-to-market plans of what products/services you'll provide to who, and how you'll reach them (achieving product-market fit).

3. A well-thought-out, simplified **plan of action**—including your order of attack and key levers.

In essence, strategy is a set of choices you make that get you set up to win—and achieve that big vision of yours.

The right structure and strategic focus combined with the right plan of action will get you on the path to seven figures in a hurry. Most entrepreneurs haven't thought very strategically about any of these three. As a result, it's made things way harder than they need to be. If that's you, we're going to change that right now.

My mission with this book is to help you get more traction in less time. The way we do this is by going deep into what we call our Model ONE™ framework. When you get this right, business and scaling become *much* easier and you'll be on the fast-track to be the leader in your niche.

There are five elements to Model ONE™, and they all fit into a single question.

Are you selling:

1. The Right People…

2. The Right Products…

3. At the Right Price…

4. With the Right Positioning…

5. In A Way That Can Scale?

Put another way, in order to grow fast to the next level, you need your target market, offer, price, positioning, and fulfillment to be simple, strategic, specific, and scalable.

Get this right, and *boom*. You are off to the races to take over your niche! Get it wrong, and you'll still be reliant on *muscling* it, feeling like you're pushing a boulder uphill when you know things should be easier.

I talk to business owners every single week, and nearly all of them think they have this figured out. I mean, they got to the first level of success, making tens of thousands or more per month, so they must be good on these elements, right?

Wrong.

Most entrepreneurs go year after year relying on muscle and grit to get clients. If even one of the five elements are off, you're going to pay for it. So let's fix this head-on and help you get true traction with your marketing by nailing your strategy.

I'm emphasizing this because I wish I knew this years ago. This is the 80/20 to get right. Using this framework would have saved me years and helped my businesses grow by many millions more. And I'm sharing this to help you do the same.

Let's break down each pillar individually now to make it happen.

Pillar 1: Where It All Begins

Entrepreneurship is solving people's problems for a profit at scale.

Read that again.

Whether you're selling marketing services, coaching, widgets, roofing, or anything else, that's what you do. You solve people's problems. At the center of all this are *people*.

More specifically, to get to the next level in your business, you need the *right* people—what we'll call your Ideal Target Audience, or *ITA* for short. You have to define who your ideal audience is and know them inside and out.

The more intimately you know and target your ITA, the more successful you'll be.

You should know their pains, dreams, desires, and fears so well that you can speak directly to them and have them think, ***"Wow, this company gets me!"***

This is important to go deep on because it's what your entire business should be built around—the ideal customers. This impacts every business decision, including:

- What products or services you provide
- What marketing channels you pick
- What marketing assets you create
- The pain points to touch on

And more.

If you are broad with your audience and try to be all things to all people like 90%+ of six-figure businesses, you'll set yourself up to fail. But if you're specific and targeted, you'll have:

- Much better conversions
- Much easier decisions
- A much simpler business
- Easier fulfillment that is more duplicable (creating much happier customers much more consistently)

And more. The answer to more traction starts with going more narrow on *WHO* you serve.

> *On a scale of 1 to 10, how clear and targeted are you on your perfect customer? Do you know them inside and out? Are you specific and clear in your marketing? Or are you casting a fairly wide net, afraid to turn away business?*

"The riches are in the niches" is a common quote for a reason. What makes this work is the specificity. The vast majority of businesses try to be too much to too broad of an audience. That doesn't work. (I know—I tried it for years!)

I get it, it's scary to shift. It's scary to get more targeted and niched. But look at it this way.

Here's how most six figure businesses look. It's a mix of ideal (ITA), ok, and pain-in-the-ass (PITA) clients.

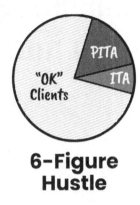

6-Figure Hustle

But imagine if you go a few layers deeper and get hyper-clear on who you're targeting, duplicating your ITA over and over while you don't let any PITA clients in.

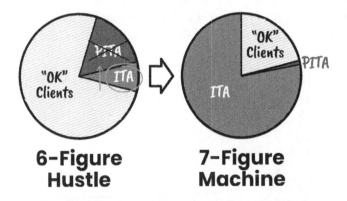

6-Figure Hustle   **7-Figure Machine**

What would this mean for your business? What about your customer experience? And how would this impact your operations and team?

I'm telling you: Everything would change on a dime.

This is one of the keys to multiple millions, and it's a decision you must make.

It drives everything.

You'll get more traction, better conversions, higher prices, more repeat-ability, happier clients, more referrals, more PR, and more.

There is a power to being #1 in your niche…and that doesn't happen if you don't get targeted!

It's called the Power Law, and essentially states that the results are not evenly distributed. In fact, they're wildly undistributed, with the leader getting a vast majority of the profits, attention, traction, and more.

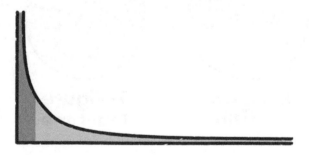

So, I know it's painful…but you must get more niched and focused. You need to go deep here.

Who is your perfect customer? Who can you best serve? Who can you be the undisputed market leader for exactly? Who would you love to duplicate as a client over and over again?

You need to define this in detail, and then back it up with ALL of your positioning, messaging, and marketing. The difference is life-changing, and the more targeted you go, the easier it'll be to scale a wildly successful business.

Our outline of 2X's ITA, who we call 'Ambitious Alex,' is 24 pages long! You can see more details on this as a guide in your 7-Figure Toolkit at 2X.co/toolkit.

Here's a short description of our ITA to show you the specificity:

Alex is 34 years old, married, and ready for the next level. They're ambitious and smart, and have had some success in a previous career. They are three years into running their own business, but now feel stuck on the 'hamster wheel' with pretty much the same problems and frustrations as a year ago. They're growing slowly (at ~$500k in revenue), but their sales are inconsistent and the business is still reliant on their time and grit—and it's getting exhausting.

They see others online thriving and growing past them, and wonder "How are they getting the traction? What am I not doing?" They know they can achieve great things—but feel trapped and over-whelmed, not reaching their potential at all.

They have five people on their core team, including their spouse who is also a partner, and three additional part-time contractors they regularly use. Their friends and family view them as successful, but they know they're really not anywhere near where they should be. They aren't paying themselves a full amount from their business, as the profits aren't consistent or repeatable. They're truly ready for a change—it has to, as it's now affecting their key relationships. Their eyes are set on finally becoming a multi seven-figure entrepreneur and living the life they envisioned for years now and they're ready to make it happen.

This is a short summary, but we go into much more depth than this. By doing so, we have more clarity on exactly who we are serving, how to market to them, what products to sell, etc. All business decisions then become much easier as we keep this perfect customer in mind.

The thing is, we aren't for everyone, and neither are you.

The key to gaining traction is to go narrow, get focused, and own your market as best you can, no matter how small that is.

Then you can start to consider going wide—but not before then. In fact, until you reach a minimum of $5 million in revenue, you shouldn't think about going wide at all.

So get clear. Get specific. Get focused. Define your ITA in detail, and then update each of the next few elements to start getting more traction than ever.

6-Figure Hustler	7-Figure CEO
• Generic and broad with your targeting	• Targeted and specific niche that you can be market leader for
• Afraid to turn business away, thinking that you'll get more business by casting a wide net	• Clear pains, desires, and customer situation deeply understood
• Don't hit on true pain points and desires, never quite emotionally connecting your marketing campaigns	• Make decisions based on this targeted ITA, and cut the rest out that is not for them
• A low portion of ITA clients and too many non-ideal or PITA clients taken on!	• Speak to this targeted ITA directly in your messaging and marketing
	• Maximize and duplicate ITA while putting restrictions in place to not work with PITA clients

Pillar 2: Your 7-Figure Product Slate

Once you know your ITA in detail, you have to really get clear and strategic about what you're selling.

Right People

Right Products

Are your products/services what your ITA *really* wants? Do you need more products or can you simplify now that you're more focused with your ITA? What is the ideal product slate to maximize customer value and growth?

With a little work, you can arrive at a pretty objective answer to help drive these questions. You just have to step back to be more strategic… and look at the data. (Shocker, I know.)

When we start with a new client at 2X, we look at:

- *Which exact offerings drive most of the sales? And profits?*
- *Which products are taking more effort than they're worth that we could cut out?*
- *Which do most of our <u>best</u> customers buy? And what's the ideal customer journey for your new ITA (to maximize LTV)?*

Nearly every business we work with, we have to adjust and optimize their product slate as they're doing too much because they have too broad of a target audience. So, start with the ITA and then let's get you the right product slate that is simple, specific, and very strategic.

Here are a few things to think about to make that happen.

1 - Identify Your Core Offer

If you don't have a core flagship offer—one that your company is known for—then you're missing out.

What is your bread and butter? What are you going to be best-in-class at? What core product can you build your business around?

Define this core offer and I'll teach you here shortly how to become the market leader for this product.

2 - Simplify To Scale

Simple scales. Period.

It's not about doing more. It's about doing less…just doing it *better*.

What can you cut out? What is not really driving big results? What products are not perfect for your new ITA that we can put on the backburner for now?

Simplifying is often one of the hardest things to do, but it's essential to get clear on what's essential and what is not. Some offerings cause more problems than they're worth. Most offerings aren't driving real impact on your bottom line. To figure out what to cut, we use a process called the *Income Stream Evaluation*, which is included in your 7-Figure Toolkit (2X.co/toolkit).

This process is simple but effective.

1. First, list all the ways you make money (your different products/ offerings).

2. Then, for each income stream, list the following estimates for the past 12 months:
   A. Revenue generated
   B. Profit margin estimate
   C. Your time involvement each month

#	Income Stream	Revenue (Last 12 Months)	Profit Margin Estimate (%)	CEO Time Per Month (Hrs)
1				
2				
3				
4				
5				

3. Then, once you have that list, go through and answer:
   Is this product ideal for your updated ITA?
   To help *you accomplish your big vision, is this offering essential?* Yes or No.

To get to seven figures fast, you have to know when to cut, maintain, or double down on an offering. When you break things down objectively this way, it's often very clear what to do. Most things are *not* essential.

Simplify first, then use the extra time, energy, and resources to optimize and scale your main moneymakers. This will lead to a lot more growth much more easily. Trust me.

3 - Don't Compete, *Differentiate*

One thing I push our private clients on daily is:

Don't compete to be better, compete to be *different!*

The vast majority of six figure entrepreneurs create products that are not differentiated from what else is out there. They're not specific, strategic, or filling a big gap. And they wonder why they aren't ever getting the traction—no matter how good their product or service is!

Is your core offering different and a better fit for your ITA than your competition's? If not, we have to make it so ASAP.

We'll talk about positioning your business and offerings in the right way here shortly, but for now, we need to map out how to make your products *irresistible* to your ITA.

4 - Make Irresistible Offers

The best thing you can do to make your marketing and sales teams look like heroes is simple: make irresistable offers that your target customer would be crazy to refuse.

Truly think about this. How can you make your products a no-brainer? How could you blow them away?

Here are seven of the key pieces of our 2X *Irresistible Offer Formula* to help you design and position your products substantially better:

1. **Pain** - You make it clear you understand your ITA's situation, pains, and challenges, and that you can address those issues head-on. The bigger the pain and desire, the more money you'll make. So start here!

2. **Specific Solution** - You make it clear you have a very specific solution that addresses your ITA's pains and goals. It's clear what you do. They don't need to understand the full process, but they need to know the solution you provide and feel like it's specifically designed for them.

3. **Differentiated Positioning** - You have strategic positioning for your company and offering that shows your ITA that you are *different* and substantially better than any alternative. You have a secret sauce and are designed specifically for your ITA.

4. **Results and Benefits** - It's clear what they receive—both tangible benefits and results, and most importantly, intangible benefits. They desperately desire those things and as a result, want your product and want it now.

5. **Value** - The perceived and actual value is substantially higher than the price, making your offer a no-brainer to the target audience. This is key. How can you make it a no-brainer by offering so much value compared to the price? And how can you position your offer so that this value is communicated? Get this right, and your sales will blow through the roof.

6. **Risk Reversal** - Take away the risk from them with a model or guarantee that addresses their biggest fears and objections and ensures you are aligned with your incentives and confident in

what you do. The right risk reversal is the icing on the cake, giving your ITA no reason but to say YES to your offer.

7. **Social Proof** - It's one thing if you sell, but another if others sell for you. The right offer is backed up with social proof, examples, and testimonials to have others show your value and benefits for you, taking away any final fears of buying.

The better you do at each element, the more likely you'll be selling more than you can handle.

To help, here is a simple process to work through, starting with your core offer:

Element	Current Rating	How To Improve
Pain		{how to make more painful, specific, and urgent to solve; relate to real-life scenario and real cost}
Specific Solution		{how to make more specific of a solution to show you are the answer for them; how to make more tangible}
Positioning		{how to be more differentiated; "Blue Ocean" positioning of offer, including what to play against—the common enemy; IP 'secret sauce' around solution}
Results/ Benefits		{how to hit on emotional level of what they truly desire; speak to the left *and* right brain}
Value		{how to stack the value to be well above the price; increase perceived value; how to add high value, low cost elements to further enhance}
Risk Reversal		{how to address their biggest fears and make it a true no-brainer}
Social Proof		{how to stack the social proof in multiple ways to attract more of your ITA, squash their fears, and show true value/impact of your offer}

Use the template in your 7-Figure Toolkit (2X.co/toolkit) as your guide, and make your offers irresistible one by one.

By doing so, you won't need a ton of products to reach seven figures. In fact, we got to our first $1 million in revenue with one single product. Remember: do less, but better.

The right product slate is simple, strategic, and specific for your ITA. Use this section to get this right and you'll have more time, profits and traction than ever. Trust me.

6-Figure Hustler	7-Figure CEO
• Multiple products that serve multiple different types of customers (often unintentionally) • No strategic ascension model • Not maximizing customer value • Offers are "ok at best" and similar to many other products in the marketplace • Too many offers, none of which are fully optimized • Hard to stand out in market, and have to compete often on price	• Strategic product slate designed to maximize customer value • Clear, targeted solutions for *ideal* customer's pains/desires—not for a broad customer base • Simplify down to the 80/20 of what matters most • *Irresistible* offers that they can't refuse, maximizing each of the seven elements above • Differentiated from the marketplace and in a category of ONE!

Pillar 3: The Price Is Right

How did you come up with your prices?

Let me guess: You picked a random number similar to other offerings in your space. Then you stick to that number for a long time (oftentimes *too* long).

It's crazy how many entrepreneurs don't strategically craft the pricing of their products—especially given its importance in impacting their bottom line. But what we need to break down is, *what is the **ideal** price of your offering?*

Let's talk about our client Ulyses (AKA U7) again to see an example of how important this is:

> At the time, Ulyses offered PR services for entrepreneurs. The price for his main program was $10,000.
>
> He was at a networking dinner with some leading online influencers (his dream clients), and they started talking about PR—where Ulyses and his business shined. This was setting up perfectly!
>
> Then Ulyses shared the price of his core package. Hearing the price of "only $10k," they all denied it right away. Since the price was off (in this case, too low), it didn't seem valuable enough, so his dream ITA dismissed it.
>
> Then, right in front of him, they asked for introductions to one of his competitors, who charged three times as much for pretty much the same value!

This price issue cost Ulyses an easy $50k in sales at that dinner, and some massive success stories with big names, which would have likely led to an additional six figures or more in future sales.

But the thing is, it's not *just* about raising your prices. Most of the time it is in fact better for you to raise your prices, but sometimes the opposite is true to make your model more scalable. We've seen success both ways. Another client recently lowered his front-end prices from $399 per month to an irresistible offer of just $19 to get more of his ITA in as customers. From there, he knew he could keep clients much longer at a lower monthly retainer ($199/mo) and thus increased his business exponentially by actually going *down* in prices.

The key is to make sure that your pricing is very strategic and intentional, and built for your perfect customer. Most don't do this but...

This one lever alone can increase your profits 40-200% pretty easily.

So start with the first two Model ONE™ elements and then let's get you priced right for your ideal audience.

Here's the process we use for a general high-ticket offer. It's a bit science and a bit art, so you're going to have to make a decision, then test and optimize it over time.

To come to a price, you need to evaluate four factors.

1 - The Floor: Cost

This may be an obvious one, but we can't be selling things (unless part of a greater strategy) for a loss. So what are your exact costs when selling something?

In service-based businesses, it's not as clear as with physical products, but that's not an excuse. You really need to know the true costs of running your business.

When determining your prices, the bottom floor is the cost. But look at the *real* cost. That means looking at everyone's time and all your overhead distributed accordingly. This is a bigger conversation than I'm going to cover here, but the better you can understand your true profitability, the more likely you will be to drive wealth and growth.

A surprising number of businesses we work with learn they have been selling one or more of their top offerings at or near a loss. And they're shocked at why they're not growing!

Spend some time to go deep and really understand the full cost of delivering one sale completely, A to Z. This clarity is painful at first, but ultimately game changing.

2 - The Roof: Value

What is the true value that someone gets from your offering? List in detail the tangible and intangible benefits and results your customers receive. How much are those things worth to your ITA? What is the *real* value of your offering if you had to put a number to it?

And most importantly…think how you can adjust your offer and positioning of the offer to maximize this perceived value. This is a key part of creating an *irresistible* offer, and the second price element to consider.

3 - The Starting Spot: Competition

Find related and competing businesses and see what they are charging. How do they price and why?

Specifically, go to those ahead of you who are where you want to be in a year or two. What are they selling their products and services for? This helps with pricing, but also much more than that.

If you aren't doing a deep-dive competitor analysis, you're missing out big time. Sam Walton, founder of Walmart, proudly claimed that he visited more retail stores than anyone else. This is so important that he didn't just send his team; he visited other competitors regularly throughout his entire career.

He was always looking for an edge, and he found it by being in the trenches, seeing what others were doing. He wanted to borrow every idea, tactic, and strategy possible—no matter how insignificant it seemed to most. He then took those ideas and shared them each week with his leadership team so they could take a lot of that and put it into action.

The result of taking the best ideas from everyone else and adding it to your own? You create the best of the best. That's what Sam and Walmart have done.

Let your competition do the hard work of validating their offerings and prices. Then you take the best among them and make something *better*.

4 - The X-Factor: Saleability

Last but not least, you have to discern how much you *could* charge your perfect customer. Given the right positioning, messaging, and value stacking, what is the price you could sell your offering over and over again to your *ideal* customer? That's the final number to take into account.

Put all four values on a chart, and use those as a guide to identify your price.

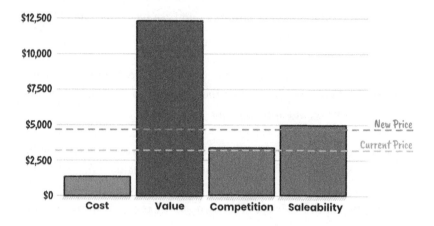

Putting all of these factors together will give you a complete picture of how to price your offering. One metric alone isn't going to cut it. All four very much matter, because:

- You'll go broke selling at or below cost.
- You can't sell above the actual and perceived value.
- Your dream customer will go elsewhere if they can get the same thing for cheaper.
- You'll have a hard time scaling if people can't pay you what you ask.

There's not some secret average or formula to this now; this is where the art comes in. But by doing this process, you're armed with the right perspective.

Also, a pro tip is: Don't just think about the price. **Think about the model and structure for how you can charge to maximize customer value.** Maybe you do a six-month minimum contract, or get paid based on results instead of a one-time charge. Or maybe you charge a setup fee to get started followed by a recurring monthly fee. Or maybe you change your program to be a full year instead of three but with a stronger guarantee, thus maximizing your LTV.

There are a lot of ways to charge, so the keys as always are:

- Stop and think very strategically to maximize your LTV.
- Think of your perfect customer, that ITA. Design the best price for them and them only. The more narrow you go, the clearer what the right price will be and the higher you can go.
- The value that you offer (real and perceived) is the key driver of price. So get strategic with your team on how to drive more value your ITA would pay for while you maximize the value:cost ratio. This is where you can exponentially grow your profits.
- The positioning of your business and irresistible offers matter so much on price, so work to dramatically improve these to back up your pricing.
- And most importantly test and iterate over time. Price is not static.

If your prices scare you a bit, that's good. That's probably the right price. Don't let fear hold you back, as more revenue and profits will help give you more opportunity to invest in a better client experience and results. And that's a true win-win.

Write these things out objectively, and you'll see that you can likely earn a lot more profit by being strategic with the right ITA targeting, model, and positioning. The right positioning makes this all so much easier to sell, so let's break that down next.

6-Figure Hustler	7-Figure CEO
• General pricing that is based on competition • Not clear on true profitability of each offering • Selling to a broad audience, so charging less than you could • Getting lots of objections on price • Doesn't strategically think about pricing model • Doesn't think about cost, customer value, and the ratio between the two	• Strategic, intentional pricing that is crafted for specific, ideal target audience • Profitability known and product slate optimized based on this • Charging based on value, not cost; maximizes this ratio to increase price, client satisfaction, and profits • Positioning backs up pricing to make *irresistible* offers

Pillar 4: Blue Ocean Positioning

Do you have competition?

Good.

That proves there is a market for what you're selling...

But I bet most of your competitors are making the same generic promises, using the same marketing strategies, and fighting over the same audience. The more noise there is in the market, the harder it is to cut through it all.

In today's competitive marketplace, it's not enough to be great. You also have to be unique.

What are the unmet and underserved needs in your niche? How are you filling a gap?

If you're familiar with the popular book, *Blue Ocean Strategy* by W. Chan Kim and Renée Mauborgne, you know to get away from the 'Red

Ocean'—where cutthroat competition fights over the same audience, turning the waters into a bloody red.

With a 'Blue Ocean,' you are essentially a category of one. **There, all competition becomes irrelevant.** To create this category of one where you are the market leader, you need to clearly define four things:

1. **Who You Are** - Identify to your core who your business is, and what makes you unique and different. What's your company's unfair advantages, skill sets or differentiators? Leverage *that*.

2. **Who You Serve** - Specifically, who is your most ideal audience, and what are the key factors that matter to them? Go back to the first step of our Model ONE framework to nail this.

3. **What You Are *The Best At*** - What are you going to choose to be known for? What can you be the best in the world at? How can you leverage this to be different from what's out there?

4. **What You *Willingly* Decide Not To Be The Best At** - You can't be the best, fastest, biggest, cheapest, etc. all in one. There have to be some trade-offs for you to be *great* at what you want to be great at, so choose wisely. And with this, you can decide who your common enemy is with your ITA. Who are you going to strategically play against to stand out even more?

The key here is, again, specificity. Going niche with your targeting *and* positioning is extremely important. It's scary. But trust me, this is very crucial in going from six to seven figures fast.

For instance, the vast majority of business-growth coaching programs are focused on marketing and sales. At 2X, however, we have seen a huge gap and filled it by focusing on what we have proven six- and seven-figure entrepreneurs *need*, which are great operations to get them free from the normal small-business hustle combined with working on things in the right order.

So we leverage that focus on systems and operations as our key differentiators, and have positioned ourselves as the best in the world at these.

Here is a 'Blue Ocean' positioning map to compare 2X versus our main competition:

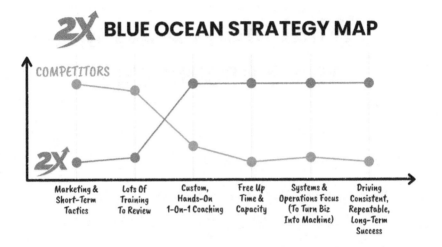

Most of our clients have tried other coaching programs and marketing gurus before, but didn't get nearly the results they wanted from that. So this is our 'common enemy' that we play against, highlighting that we do NOT focus on those same things. When they see that we approach things in a different way and we show them why the other approach doesn't work, we can quickly train them the right way, thus putting us in the power position to help them.

Using our example as a guide, I highly recommend you create your own 'Blue Ocean' map. What are the key factors that make you different? See a training and template on this in your 7-Figure Toolkit (2X.co/toolkit).

Let others compete on the same topics, while you create your own category of ONE. Leverage your unique greatness, and become known for something that matters to your ITA. This leads to more referrals and word-of-mouth marketing, more loyalty, better conversions, and ultimately, more growth.

So how are you going to be positioned?

What are you going to be known for?

To help, start with:

What is in your DNA (natural zone of genius) that you're going to be the best in the world at?

Where are your competitors weak—where you can excel?

What are your key differentiators to set you apart?

What are you going to be known for? What word/phrase/topic do you want to own in your niche?

Get clear. Get specific. Choose what you're going to be the best at. And strategically position yourself in a *category of one*. It's priceless when you do.

6-Figure Hustler	7-Figure CEO
• In a crowded marketplace of similar companies and offers • Not differentiated from competition; very similar to other brands and offers • Trying to be good at too many things (when in reality you can't be!); afraid to pick what you're bad at	• Strategic positioning that is specifically designed for ITA • Different (and better) than ITA's other alternatives • Key differentiating factors defined and emphasized by brand • Strategically choose what you *won't* do and offer so that you can do the main things really well • Leverages your differentiating factors in your marketing to turn away non-ITA clients and attract more ideal ones • Chooses a common enemy to play against to better emphasize what really matters to your ITA

Pillar 5: In A Way That Can Scale

If you implement the Model ONE™ elements discussed so far, you'll be setting your business up for success. But here's the kicker:

You can have an amazing offering that is targeted to the right audience, easy to sell, profitable, and creating raving fan customers, but...

If your business is still built around you and your time, then it is not a true business.

And it's definitely not scalable.

You will hit a ceiling on your growth and a wall with your energy. Trust me, I've been there. I was stuck for years at six figures and burned out more times than I'd like to admit.

I had built my business around me, my time and talent, and as a result, I worked myself to the bone trying to scale. I was so exhausted and overwhelmed that I started having anxiety attacks. Every time I drifted off to sleep, I would gasp up in bed to breathe—praying that I'd make it to be alive in the morning.

I had this so bad that I had to call 911 to make sure I wasn't dying. Then I learned, there's a much better, smarter way—and one that actually is a key to growth too.

So here's the fifth and final piece of the Model ONE™ framework:

Make sure your business is designed to run and scale *without* you—or any other key person or resource.

To do so, we need to see your business as a scalable machine. Not a self-employed job reliant on your talent.

How can you turn it into a machine that thrives without you? That's what our entire 2X *Machine Methodology* is about.

You got into business because you're smart, capable, good at what you do, and you wanted more control over your income, growth, impact, and opportunities. Since starting your business, you've reached that first level of success by driving the show through grit and determination.

But to really scale and to finally get what you *really* want—the freedom, the income, the impact, the opportunities—we have to change this. We have to stop having the business centered around you.

This graphic is what most six-figure businesses org charts look like, whether you want to admit it or not.

Now, don't get me wrong:

You can still be the face. You can still be the CEO. You can still do your magic—the thing that got you to this point, the 'art' you enjoy doing. **But to grow fast, you cannot have your business *require* you day-in and day-out.**

If it does, then you're limited. Your time is limited. Your energy is limited. Your brain capacity is limited. And your growth will be limited. That's not what you want.

So, you need the proper team, structure, systems, and operations to have your business be able to run fine without you. **That is when you are *truly* scalable.**

We'll break this all out in detail so you can get free, but start to brainstorm what needs to happen to have your business run just fine without you. How can you make your fulfillment be much more scalable? What operations and team changes do you need to make?

Start to think about these things, and we'll get clear on the key steps in the next two chapters.

I know the thought of removing yourself can be scary at first. But it's necessary. Either you get ahead of it, or you wait until you hit a wall.

So, are you ready to unlock growth? Then it's time to be courageous and let go.

6-Figure Hustler	7-Figure CEO
• Business built around you and your talents • Team dependent on feedback, direction, approval, and ideas from you • You're essentially trading time for money • Can't effectively handle a lot more customers; not scalable in current form	• Business built to scale *without* you (or any one key person) • CEO fully removed from the day-to-day operations • Can handle more customers at scale • Has repeatable delivery process to make clients raving fans

Your Growth Lever (To Millions)

Now that we've shared the five pillars of Model ONE™, let's get into a few other key elements of having a seven-figure strategy and model to be set up for success, starting with a key growth hack that most don't take advantage of.

Whether you're at $200k per year—or $500k, $5 million, or somewhere in between—here's a lesson I never want you to forget:

> One of your best growth levers—something that will make your life way better and your bank account way fuller—is to maximize the lifetime value (LTV) of a customer.

If a customer buys from you one time for $1,000, then their LTV is $1,000.

If they buy one product from you for $1,000, and another service for $200 per month for six months, then their LTV is $2,200 ($1,000 + 6 x $100). Same customer, just a lot more revenue.

One of the hardest and most expensive things in business is to get new customers. So when you do, *keep* them!

With this one lever alone, you can dramatically grow your business.

There are four key ways to impact your LTV:

1. Raise your prices (or go higher-end)

2. Sell your customers more *new* stuff (cross-sell or upsell)

3. Sell your customers more of the *same* stuff (and keep them longer!)

4. Adjust your business model, the structure of how you get paid, and/or offerings

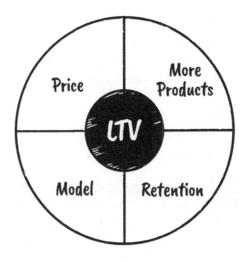

Oftentimes, we'll do a combination of these to drive higher LTV. This is such an important key to growth that we address this on day one with all new clients.

Most of the time, it only takes a couple of simple tweaks to multiply their customers' LTV by two to four times. This way, we don't even have to talk about going out and finding new customers, spending money on advertising, or doing much more work. With one simple lever you can 2-4x your business!

The power of this can't be underestimated.

Remember: one of the most expensive things in business is to acquire new customers, so get very strategic, intentional, and skilled at maximizing the value of the ones you do get.

Consider the following questions to help:

>*What changes can you make to enhance your customers' LTV? Can you sell them more products or raise your prices?*

>*How can you keep your customers twice as long?*

>*Can you change how you charge to get even more revenue long-term?*

>*Map out the perfect customer journey for your ideal target customer. What is the perfect flow of products to maximize their LTV?*

Once you've given those questions some thought, map out this structure with your conservative target goals. This will be your product map, and the blueprint to many millions of dollars done right.

6-Figure Hustler	7-Figure CEO
• Focuses much more on trying to get more new leads and customers over everything else • Thinks that *more leads* is the solution that will solve all of their problems • Focuses more on the sale than the customer • Doesn't maximize customer value	• Strategically designed business and offerings to maximize LTV • Understand that raving fans are at the heart of a great business; and much easier path to growth • Strategically crafts the four key drivers: price, products, retention, and model

Three Buckets Of Great Strategy

STRATEGY is the 80/20. Get this right, and everything else is easy.

One of the key things I want you to take away from this book is to shift from the idea of hustling hard to scale…to be strategic and intentional. Strategy is the 80/20 of growth.

A simple system we use to help make sure you're set up to scale for the long-term is our Three-Buckets Strategy.

What we're going to do is think of your business in three time frames:

1. **Right Now**: the next 30 days
2. **Medium-Term**: 6 to 12 months from now
3. **Long-Term**: 3 to 5 years out

Many entrepreneurs are stuck trying to merely survive, so they aren't thinking strategically about anything past hitting payroll and this month's bills. However, if you have a strategic plan for each of these three buckets and execute on each, you are going to shift more and more away from the 'Right Now' bucket…

And soon after, you'll be a *very* successful entrepreneur. The more you can get ahead and work on the key levers that will set you up 3, 6, 12 months from now, the more that you will start to see exponential long-term growth.

Let's look at a few questions to consider for each time frame so you can be more strategic and intentional than ever.

Bucket 1 - Right Now:

Do you have a strategy in place to hit your short-term leads and sales targets?

Do you have the cash on hand to cover all expenses (and more), and not worry about having to be reactive? Are you set for the next 30-plus days so you can focus on the longer-term strategic actions?

And are you clear on the highest impact things you can do this week and month to drive you towards your quarterly and annual targets and initiatives? Reverse-engineer those big levers to a specific action plan that you and your team can execute right now.

Bucket 2 - Medium-Term:

Are you clear on the highest impact levers you need to achieve in the next 3-6 months that will get you on the fast-track to your bigger vision? Is your team clear and aligned on these too?

Are the actions you and your team are taking this month setting your business up for six-plus months down the line?

One of my favorite questions to ask is: *Six months from now, what will you wish you had done right now?* Make sure you do that!

Bucket 3 - Long-Term:

Do you have a clear vision of where your business will be a few years down the line? Are you clear on the key strategic moves and actions that are going to get you there? And is your team clear and aligned on this?

Are you strategic and intentional about your vision, with the right strategy and model?

And do you use this vision as your guide to see what is not essential and what you should be focusing on?

Think through and write out your response to each one of these.

Each bucket is so important because

The fact of the matter is the future arrives faster than you think.

Six months go by in the blink of an eye. And before you know it, three years flies by as well.

It's the businesses that strategically plan ahead and make sure that the steps they're taking align with the long-term vision that are the ones who will win.

More and more, your time should be spent on the medium-term levers— the things that are super important but *not* that urgent. Those are your real moneymakers. Those are the main actions that will make an impact and get you where you want to go. Yet most six figure entrepreneurs stay stuck focused mostly on the short-term.

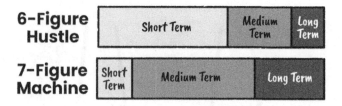

It's not about being busy. It's about being strategic and intentional. So spend the time, get clear on your long term first, then the key medium term levers, then down to the highest impact short term stepping stones that will get you off of the six figure hamster wheel once and for all.

Your future self will thank you for it.

6-Figure Hustler	7-Figure CEO
• Focused primarily on the short-term *survival mode* actions	• Strategic alignment working backwards from the vision with clear short-term and high level medium-term milestones and initiatives
• Many actions spending time on aren't in clear alignment with the long-term vision	• Very intentional and strategic series of steps towards big goals/vision
• Team isn't clear on the progression of steps to get to the big vision	• Moving away from short-term actions into more medium- and long-term actions, knowing this is where the big results come from
• Busy but not strategic or intentional	• Team is clear and aligned on progression of steps and how everything builds up toward the vision

The Million-Dollar Question

Prepping to start 2X a few years ago, I took some time to compare my friends who were absolutely crushing it, scaling to big numbers quickly, to those who have potential but are stagnant or stuck on the hamster wheel.

What's the difference? What do the most successful do that the unsuccessful don't?

I came to this conclusion:

The most successful compress time!

They are always thinking, *"How can I get this accomplished as easily and quickly as possible?"*

They're looking to **accomplish in 60 days what most do in six months** and are constantly searching for the shortest path. They know the power (and price) of time, speed, and opportunity cost—things that those doing "okay" never quite value enough.

The average person is looking to save pennies, while the best are looking to make *big money moves*. The average person is looking to figure it out themselves and do even more, while the best are trying to do less with more *leverage*.

Knowing this, I created the *million-dollar question* that we use internally at 2X and with our private clients every day. It simply asks:

"What's the simplest and most direct path?"

Got a big project you want to complete? Great. What's the *simplest and most direct path* to get it done?

Want to take your qualified leads from ten per week to forty per week? Great. What's the simplest and most direct path to make that happen?

Want to get your business from six to seven figures? Again, what's the simplest and most direct path?

This question is worth well more than a million bucks. It's ingrained in our heads, and I hope it becomes your go-to question as well because you know that strategy is the 80/20 of growth. And a secret hack to great strategy: it's SIMPLE.

This million-dollar question will guide you to make it as simple and strategic as possible.

The answer to *more*—more money, more time, more freedom, more consistency, more *growth*—is through less. So, start by figuring out what the goal is...

Then ask the million-dollar question:

"What's the simplest and most direct path?"

Get more strategic. Compress time. And start blowing past your goals. The next chapter will help make sure that happens. It's the "tipping point" where everything changes in your business.

6-Figure Hustler	7-Figure CEO
• Tries to add on more and more to do • Thinks more complex is better • Thinks they can get everything done in an ambitious period of time	• Knows that *simple* is the key to a great strategy and plan • Always thinking how to simplify, cutting out what is not essential • Realizes that things will take longer than we think, so takes on much less • Gets clear on goals, vision and outcomes...and then thinks, *"what is the simplest and most direct path to make that a reality?"* • Trains others to also think with this mentality

Chapter 2 Big Ideas

- Model ONE™ is your guide to a better, simpler business and more traction than ever.
  - o Are you selling the right people, the right products, at the right price, with the right positioning in a way that can scale? If you are clear, targeted, and strategic with this, you'll be the market leader in no time. But most are not!
- It all begins by getting more targeted on who you serve; your *ideal* target audience. Your entire business will change the more clear and targeted you get here. You want to become the clear market leader for this ITA.
- From there, craft the strategic product slate to help you maximize customer value and conversions by making truly irresistible offers. This makes everything else easier.
- Maximizing LTV is often the single best lever to grow! Think critically on this, and your entire business (and profits) will change. The four key drivers are: price, products, retention, and model.
- Strategically craft the right prices and you can increase your profits 50-200% fairly quickly. Think about maximizing the value while also optimizing costs so your ratio of value to cost goes up. This makes it easy to raise your prices and profits exponentially.
- Don't compete to be better. Compete to be *different* and stand out from your competition, planting your flag in the marketplace. Your positioning is key.
- Get clear alignment between short, medium and long-term actions to get on the fast-track towards your vision. Cut out everything that is not in alignment to get you to your big vision and goals.
- Move away from the constant short-term reactive focus. Your real money makers are the non-urgent key actions that will show up in results in the medium- and long-term.
- Get clear on what outcomes you want…and then use the Million Dollar Question as your guide: *What's the simplest and most direct path?*

CHAPTER 3

FIRE YOURSELF FROM THE DAY-TO-DAY

The One Thing Holding Your Business Back

Before you can scale, we need to have a little chat.

There's *one thing* that is stopping you from your goals and the success you know is possible. It's making things way harder than they need to be, and holding back your business, your income, your freedom, your team, and you from reaching your potential.

Unfortunately, that one thing is *you*. You are the bottleneck.

Don't worry, you're not alone. Almost every entrepreneur we work with is the one holding things back, and I've been there more times than I'd like to admit.

Not only do we mentally hold ourselves back with fear, our mindset, or self-sabotage, but specifically, in your business, *you are the bottleneck*. You are likely being pulled in so many different directions, wearing too many hats, and responsible for everything from marketing to finances, team to client success. It's no wonder you don't have time to drive real growth!

We have to change that.

And we will.

So, it's time to fire yourself from the day-to-day operations. It's time to step into your role as CEO and be working "on" the business, not stuck working "in" it.

The thing is, in small businesses, there are a lot of moving pieces. You're going to be responsible for a lot. So, the constraint to solve for is your time. If we get this right, and you get free from the weeds of your business, everything changes.

That's why we call this the tipping point. That's what this chapter is about, to help you get free so that you can grow AND live your best life. So let's take back control of your time and get you free.

6-Figure Hustler	7-Figure CEO
• Stuck in the day-to-day operations, pulled in 100 directions • Neverending to-do list • Exhausted and overwhelmed	• Working "on" the business, not stuck "in" it • In control of time and calendar with a clear focus on what matters most

The Two-Week Vacation Test

If you went on a two-week vacation right now—100% off the grid, with no internet and zero connection to your email or team—*what would happen to your business?*

What about your income? Your clients? And most importantly, how would you *feel?*

Would you be on the beach, toes in the sand, without a care in the world? Or would your little vacation morph into two weeks of stress as you **try** to enjoy family time but can't stop thinking about all that you have to do in business?

Most business owners would have to admit it looks more like the latter.

Here at 2X, that is *not* okay with us. One of our core values is "Level 10 Life," which means being balanced, having fun, putting family first, and creating experiences to live an amazing life. Business is just part of it.

We help make sure our entire company has that freedom and balance, and we're here to help you do the same. I mean, what is all the work worth if you can't enjoy it?

So, not only can this two-week vacation test tell you the true health of your business, but time off helps you recharge your energy and clear your mind. This allows you to think more strategically and make better decisions, so, ultimately, going on vacation isn't just good for balance, it's often great for business and is most definitely powerful for your team, as well.

Now, as you go on that no-strings-attached vacation, one of four things will happen to your business. And this is a huge sign of the health of your business:

- **Level 1**: Your business would fail pretty quickly without you.
- **Level 2**: Your business would slowly fail and start to fall apart without your direction and work.
- **Level 3**: Things would be able to operate okay without you for a few weeks.
- **Level 4**: Your business would still thrive and be able to grow without you!

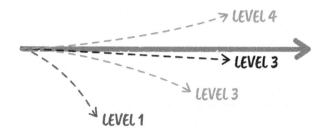

Level 4 is obviously where you want to be.

This book is all about getting you to grow with consistency and control, but also to most importantly do so with you taking back control of your time.

We have had so many clients go from working every weekend, never taking any time off, to having a completely different life in the first few weeks working with us. By following the suggestions we've outlined in this book, they've created growing businesses—that can run and thrive *without* them. This is when you're in the power position!

Our 2X client Erin hadn't taken a weekend or week off in 20 years in business. Seriously. Read that again! No weekends off in twenty years. Now she takes every weekend off, and has enjoyed three *full* weeks off in her first four months with us.

Liz just got back from a 12-day trip to Dubai and only spent one hour on work. She now has plans for doing these trips monthly, even with her business growing fast from the mid-six to now seven figures.

Kyle and his wife Christie got back from a vacation to Hawaii where Kyle was present on vacation for "the first time in forever," per Christie. Oh, and they made $170k in those two weeks (which is up dramatically from $88k per month pre-2X) with only four to five hours of work. They've now gone on to multiple millions.

So how did they do it?

And how can *you* get your business 'vacation-ready'?

Here are three things that are necessary to get you ready for that much-needed, 100% off, relaxing and rewarding vacation:

1 - Simplify

Business can be tough as hell. There's so much to take into account. To get the most out of your time—and to give you that vacation you've been wanting—you need to simplify the business down to **what really matters** and cut out what doesn't. This is one of your top responsibilities as CEO.

> *What's the 80/20 of your business? What is essential? And most importantly, what is not essential that you can cut out to better set your team and business up for success?*

Look at your products, marketing strategies, projects going on, etc. and SIMPLIFY. The better you do at this, the more likely you'll reach seven figures fast.

'Simple and strategic' is the secret to seven figures.

You only have 24 hours in a day, and you definitely don't want to spend 18 of them working. So take the time each and every week to think how you can make things easier. What can you cut out or push off to a later date? Take some time this week to do a deep review of what is essential. It's scary at first, but also liberating to do less.

Trust me, this will mean good things for your business.

2 - Model

As we discussed in Chapter 2, most entrepreneurs start their business around them because that's all they have. But to make the leap, you have to change your structure. Your company should not be built around you—or reliant on any one person, for that matter.

Not only does this allow you to scale to much higher levels, but—you guessed it—you can step out for vacation and have things run smoothly without you!

Design your business to drive what you really want—growth and freedom—and set yourself up for success. Otherwise, you'll be creating even more work and headaches as you try to scale.

So, where is your business tied to your time? Where are things reliant on you?

Create an action plan to systemize and delegate all responsibilities that could stop you from being fully removed from the day-to-day operations (which I'll show you how to soon).

And last but not least, to get free from the weeds once and for all, you need:

3 - Systems

At the center of your business machine are systems.

Systems are your single greatest form of *leverage* in your business.

If you have the right systems in place for each part of your Value Chain (more on that soon), you have more repeatability, consistency, scalability, and most importantly, you have a mechanism you can delegate to someone else.

Do this enough times and your business won't need you!

Adopting systems and getting you free from your business requires a mindset shift, though. In school or in a job, or even when starting out in business, we're taught to make ourselves irreplaceable. Our egos get a dopamine hit out of being *needed*. We feel special and important. We have a purpose! So subconsciously, whether we realize it or not, we teach ourselves to keep our business needing us. Our ego loves when we are the smartest, or when our clients need us.

But the path to success and freedom in business means doing the opposite:

Creating the structures and systems for a company that *doesn't* need you.

Once you're in this position, you can truly work "on" the business, do the things that truly grow it, start earning more money than ever before, and…You can take as many vacations as you want (for as long as you want) and finally be able to 100% relax when you do!

This isn't a fairytale. This is what's possible. We see it day-in and day-out with private clients. And frankly, it's good for your business.

The uncapped upside *and* true time freedom to do what you want when you want is a big part of why you got into business to begin with, so let's get you free…and schedule that vacation!

6-Figure Hustler	7-Figure CEO
• Unable to fully step away as your business is reliant on you • Business would slowly fail without you, so you can't take a real break • Team isn't empowered or able to work properly without entrepreneur support and guidance	• Business can run and thrive without them • Able to take relaxing time off, knowing the business will be fine • Uses vacations and time off strategically to improve the team and business

Stop Being A Superhero

When you're a kid, being a superhero is awesome. You put on the cape and can be anyone you want to be.

But in your business? Not so much.

Sure, you can go through spikes of energy where everything feels fresh and new, sending you into do-it-all superhero mode. But those energy spikes usually don't last long, and soon enough, you'll find yourself exhausted and burnt out.

I've been there, wearing so many hats and trying to be a superhero entrepreneur for years! I was the one to work with the clients, do the strategy, do the sales, manage my small team, write emails, handle customer service questions from my team, put out fires, follow up on failed payments, lead meetings, deal with the finances, and more.

It was exhausting—and a flat-out dumb idea that led to me having to call 911 not once, but twice with anxiety attacks!

The good news is, I learned there is a better, *simpler* way. And this book is a guide into that.

But one interesting thing I've found is, not only is it better for your lifestyle, mindset, health, and family to get free from the weeds of your business. It's also a major secret to growth!

Remember, only 4% of people get past that magic $1 million per year mark. And only a tenth of that group make it past $10 million per year!

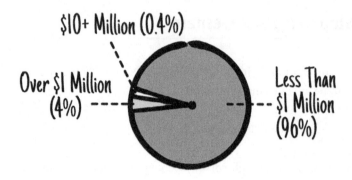

$10+ Million (0.4%)

Over $1 Million (4%)

Less Than $1 Million (96%)

Why such low numbers?

It's because of this fact: most entrepreneurs are stuck working "in" the day-to-day operations.

Most are trying to do too much themselves, and really are trading time for money.

Is this the case for you?

It's time to put an end to the games and give up *trying* or even *thinking* you can do it all. Instead, start being a seven-figure CEO.

- One who is working on high-leverage activities, not stuck doing admin tasks.
- One who is spending time on growth, not putting out fires every day.
- One who is in control of their time and actions, not reactive to each situation.
- One who is solving issues at the source (with people and systems), not doing everything themselves.

To get to seven figures, you have to figure out what few things you will own—that is, what responsibilities will you have in your business? What are your key swimlanes (as one of our 2X Coaches Dr. Kristin Kahle calls them) that you'll spend most of your time on? And that leads to an even tougher question:

What things will you NOT own? What will you fire yourself from?

Everyone on your team should have three to five core role responsibilities max, and the first role to define is yours. Then, once you're clear on this, ideally eighty percent of your time in these key high-impact swimlanes.

That may be a far cry from where you're at now, but let's get back to what we explored at the beginning of the book. **In an ideal world, how would you spend your time to help you accomplish your vision as fast as possible?** What are the top responsibilities you need to own that will have the highest impact?

Odds are you aren't spending enough time on these things now, but the first step is defining where your time should go. Odds also are that you're working hard enough, we just need to get focused on the right activities.

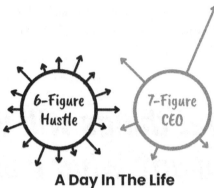

A Day In The Life

As an example, here are my top responsibilities:

Strategic Vision - Setting the overall company vision and direction, making sure everyone is clear and aligned to move fast towards our vision.

Building a World-Class Team - Hiring, leading, and optimizing an elite team and culture and helping make sure everyone is set up for success.

Head of Growth - Spearheading the strategy for our key marketing and growth initiatives, and ensuring all department actions lead up to our growth goals.

Strategic Partnerships - Creating alliances with companies and brands for win-win relationships.

Asset Marketing Creation - Creating things like this book, video series, podcasts, and other marketing assets that will be leveraged to reach a big audience over and over again.

I spend 80% or more of my time on these tasks. Not only is this the best use of my time, but leading and driving growth while creating some content is exactly what I want to do.

You, too, can design whatever you want in your business. Just make sure that all of the key responsibilities are clearly owned by someone, otherwise you'll have to jump in and own those yourself.

Some of the most common CEO income-producing activities we suggest are:

1. To create, maintain, and evolve the strategic vision and direction of the business—your team needs to see and feel where you're headed, as this 'North Star' guides all of the decisions and creates more than just a 'job' for people.
2. Lead growth and your overall strategy to scale.
3. Be the spokesperson of the business leading the marketing and content.
4. Focus on mass sales opportunities (reaching the masses and optimizing your time).
5. Growing and optimizing a world-class team by recruiting, hiring, onboarding, training, and developing your employees.
6. Form strategic partnerships with others who have an audience of potential buyers of your products/services to create a win-win.
7. Managing and optimizing finances and capital to drive growth.
8. Acquiring other businesses to include or leverage to exponentially grow your own.
9. Creating a best-in-class scalable product/program.
10. New product development and extensions.
11. Spearheading the biggest bottleneck initiative at any time.

Brainstorm the top responsibilities you need to embrace to expand your business.

What is the best and highest-impact use of your time?

What are the key responsibilities you need to adopt to get to seven figures?

What do you enjoy doing that you still want to own?

And a question I love to consider is,

If you only had 10 hours per week to manage your business, what would you do?

Start there.

Brainstorm a list, and then trim it down to the top five swimlanes.

Remember: It's time to stop being a do-it-all superhero. Get clear and step into your role as a seven figure CEO. It's time.

6-Figure Hustler	7-Figure CEO
• Trying to do "it all" yourself to cut corners and save time in the short-term	• Clear on highest-impact role, including what you will and will *not* do
• No defined role or responsibilities	• Defined role and swimlanes
• On the fast-track to burn out by taking on too much	• Spending 80%+ of your time on highest impact role, cutting out and delegating the rest effectively
• Too much time spent on low-impact activities	• Clear on the value of your time and protect it that way

Simple 7-Figure Org Chart

I love the Winston Churchill quote, *"For the first 25 years of my life, I wanted freedom. For the next 25 years, I wanted order. For the next 25 years, I realized that order is freedom."*

It's a wise lesson to learn that order is freedom. Structure isn't restricting. Done right, it's the exact thing that will get you the freedom you want.

So, one of the structures we need is an org chart, listing out the key roles, departments, and who reports to who. You can make it all fancy and detailed, or you can just keep things really simple (and you know what we'd recommend!).

No matter how your business is currently structured, here's the 80/20 roles to fill. We call it the Simple 7-Figure Org Chart:

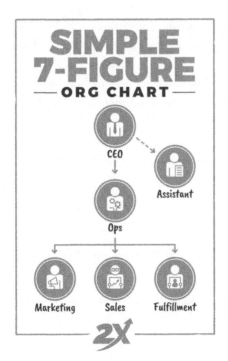

There are six major roles to be filled. We just have to make sure they aren't all filled by you!

Starting out in your business, you do everything. From top to bottom, your name is on every part of the org chart. But over time, you have to remove yourself from nearly everything so you can work "on"—and actually grow—your company with one hat on: The CEO.

The six core functions for most businesses are:

CEO - The leader of vision and high-level strategy.

Operations (Ops) - The one who helps keep you out of the weeds and oversees the machine that is (or will be) your business.

Marketing - Driving lead generation and creating sales opportunities.

Sales - Overseeing sales conversions and the sales team to make sure you're converting the leads at the highest level.

Fulfillment - The client services making sure you fulfill on the promises made, turning customers into raving fans, and executing your delivery.

Assistant - Handling so much of the administrative tasks involved in business.

All six are critical.

Here are a few things to think about with this org chart as you scale past $1M in revenue.

1 - You Can Only Be In Two *Max*

You can be CEO and the department manager of one major function.

Try to do more than that and things start to fall through the cracks. Then you get overwhelmed and frustrated, and nobody wins.

Full ownership of a department means owning the strategy, numbers, execution, and results of that part of your business. As you scale quickly to seven figures, you just won't be able to manage it all for more departments!

So pick your two functions that you'll own—or better yet, fire yourself from everything and only be in the CEO position.

2 - Get Each Department Seven-Figure Worthy

For each role, make sure you evaluate whether the department owner is seven-figure caliber.

Is this the person and talent that is going to get you to the next level?

So often we put people in roles just because we have them, but that doesn't mean they are the people we *need*. They may be strong to help get you to one level of success, but are they the ones who will help you get to the next level as fast and easily as possible?

For example, the team that got us to seven figures at 2X is not the same as what we need for eight figures, so we've been making the necessary changes to key positions to help us make that next leap as a company.

So, review your team in detail and be honest with yourself. Do you have the people at each of these six main functions to get you to seven figures fast?

If not, it's time to make a game plan to hire and build your world-class team. The thing is...

3 - Start With *One*

How do you eat an elephant? *One* bite at a time.

How do you build a machine that can thrive without you? *One* system and person at a time.

How should you fill these six roles and build an elite team? You guessed it, *one* person at a time.

Trying to hire more than one person or make a bunch of team changes all at once is a recipe for disaster. I've tried it countless times, and it leads to worse recruiting, hiring, onboarding, and leads to a crazy low likelihood of success.

So, use this Simple 7-Figure Org Chart as your guide to start to think about who you'll hire next.

6-Figure Hustler	7-Figure CEO
• No defined/updated org chart of who reports to who • Business really built around you • Maybe one other key driver of results on your team, but most results are still reliant on you • Don't have a rockstar assistant • Tries to hire multiple roles at once without setting them up to succeed	• Defined and updated org chart with team clear on who reports to who • Other key leaders in place driving results and taking off responsibilities from you • Free from the weeds, in max of one other non-CEO role • Rockstar assistant in place keeping you out of admin tasks • Clear hiring plan with one key role at a time to set them up to succeed

The Value Of Your Time

The major differentiator between six figures and multiple millions is how you value, protect, and spend your time.

How you spend your time is the ultimate leading indicator.

And the thing is, not all time is created equal. In fact, it's wildly disproportionate.

To make big changes to your revenue and wealth, we have to level up the value of your time.

Let's say you want to take home $500,000 in personal earnings this year (total of salary and distributions). And let's say you work on average 40 hours per week and 50 weeks per year (two off for vacations and holidays). So, this would mean that your earnings need to be $250 per hour. That is the average.

So for every hour you spend doing $10 per hour admin activities, you need to replace that with a ~$500 per hour activity.

So how much do you want to make? Let's get clear on what the value of your time needs to be using this calculation:

$$\frac{\text{Target Earnings}}{\text{Hours Per Week} \times \text{Weeks Worked Per Year}} = \text{Average Value of Time (\$/Hour)}$$

From here, you can see what you need to let go of. The key thing is to offload as much at the bottom end and increase your high-impact time. One way we think about it is with the *2X Delegation Rule*, which states that you should delegate anything and everything that is less than half of your hourly rate.

So if your rate needs to be $250 per hour (per the above example), then you should work to offload anything and everything that you can hire out for under $125 per hour. And do you know how much you can offload and delegate for under $125 per hour? Pretty much anything!

Now, let's make this tangible. Here's a chart that lists out some examples of how you could spend your time.

$10 Per Hour	$100 Per Hour	$1,000 Per Hour	$5,000+ Per Hour
Posting On Social Media	Writing Blog Post Or Email	Big Marketing Initiative	Nailing Model ONE™ Elements
Fixing Website	Leading Day-To-Day Meetings	Creating A System For Client Success	Creating An Irresistible Offer
Running Errands	Working With Clients	Problem Solving With Department Manager	Hiring Key Leadership Role

It's easy to get busy on $10 or $100 per hour tasks. This is where you're comfortable. It's safe here, and what got you to this point.

But it's time for the next level, so we have to up-level the tasks that you work on.

This is important to write out, so use the table in your 7-Figure Toolkit (2X.co/toolkit) and fill in the tasks you can think of for each level for your business. The first step to change anything is awareness, so write it down and you'll start to notice more often when you're busy on the bottom end.

Next, let's get you free from all of those tasks holding you back!

6-Figure Hustler	7-Figure CEO
• Don't know the value of your time • Is busy, but mostly on low-end tasks • Tries to cut corners and thinks "it's better if I just do it myself" rather than offloading tasks • More comfortable doing $100 per hour and less tasks, as that's what you're familiar with • Afraid to let go	• Knows and protects the value of their time • Fiercely offloads anything under $100 per hour • Clear on the highest impact responsibilities • Every quarter working to increase the value of how you spend your time

Delegate Like A Boss With XDS™

Remember the goal:

Eighty percent of your time should be spent on your top high-impact activities.

To get there, odds are you have to offload potentially dozens of other tasks. So where do you start? With a process I do every single month. We call it the **XDS™ System**.

Using the action guide in your 7-Figure Toolkit (found at 2X.co/toolkit), here's how to execute this system and free up 10-20 hours per week in a hurry.

Take this seriously and complete this exercise as you go. Here's how to do it:

Step 1: List ALL Of The Tasks

Think of the past two weeks, and list out *all* of the tasks you spent your time and energy on that may come up again. Detail every thing you can think of, as the better you do at this step it'll make everything else easier to actually offload. For instance, don't write something general like 'social media.' Instead, be more granular: 'creating social media content' and 'engaging in business Facebook groups.'

Even if something has taken a total of 30 minutes combined in the last month, include it.

Seriously, take some time and do this. I block off at least 15 minutes to write down every task, small or big. You can see an example in your 7-Figure Toolkit too that will help.

Step 2: Add The Time Estimate

Now put the estimated average time per week that you spend on each task. Be honest—nobody else is seeing this besides you. Where is your time going? List that out, and you'll start to see that it's pretty eye-opening that so much time is *not* going towards the highest impact activities.

Specific Task	Time (Hrs/Wk)
Leading Team Meetings	2.5
New Client Setup+Welcome	1.5
Creating Social Media Content For Week	3.0
Creating Strategic Partnerships	4.5

Step 3: Identify Each Task Tier

Then you need to categorize each task into tiers based on level of importance. Here are the four tiers with example tasks for each:

Tier 1: Admin - Email inbox, social media posting, simple tech, customer service, setting up blog posts

Tier 2: Technician - Doing 'the work,' low-level project management, client delivery, editing and optimizing web pages, basic content creation, prospecting, sales

Tier 3: Manager - Team management, employee optimization, running meetings, legal, creating systems

Tier 4: Executive - Strategy, leading big marketing initiatives, hiring key roles, building partnerships

Don't overthink it as you go through each task. Just fill in your best guess for which tier fits, as this lays the groundwork for what's to come.

Step 4: Evaluate Your Energy

Now you need to evaluate how you feel about each task. Does it give you energy? Does it sap your energy?

Now you want to go through your tasks and put:

- An up arrow (◪) next to tasks that *give* you energy
- A down arrow (◪) next to tasks that *take* energy
- Or a dash (-) for tasks that are neutral

For me, I love creating pillar content assets such as this book. That gets me excited and gives me energy (◪).

But doing tech tasks and fixing landing pages? Not so much. That drains me (◪).

Go through and review each item. And now the fun part…

Step 5: Fire Yourself!

Now it's time to get you free with XDS™, by cutting (X), delegating (D), and systemizing (S) all of the tasks that you don't want to or shouldn't own. With this simple method, you'll get a lot off your plate, so here's how to do it:

X - Cut

The best and fastest way to free up time is to cut things out. Most things are not essential, so lean into this.

Once more, go through your list and ask these important questions:

- *What is on this list that we can just cut out altogether?*
- ***What is just not essential?***
- *What things, if we cut them, wouldn't make that big of a difference to our business and growth (besides freeing up time and energy!)?*

For items that fit any of those criteria, mark X beside them and then cross out that entire row. Those are the items we're going to cut out.

I get it, it's scary to cut things out. But every single time we've done this process with clients and really dive in, we see a lot of things that are not essential. We often find 20-40% of their tasks that they can completely cut out altogether. At a minimum, find 10% of your time that should be cut.

D - Delegate

Next, excluding all of the X'ed items, add a "D" for which items to delegate. These will include:

- All tasks you don't enjoy doing (that take your energy)
- All tasks you *shouldn't* be doing (like admin and technician tasks) that you don't love
- And all tasks that someone else can do (whether you have that person on your team now or that you can hire for)

That will take care of a good portion of your list, as a *lot* of things you're doing can be done by someone else, especially when you give them the proper support.

S - Systemize

Now, go through the items that aren't X'ed off and put an S beside the ones you need to create or improve a system for.

(Note: Some of the items you're going to delegate will need a system before you can hand it off, so you'll have some items with a D and S at the same time. This won't always be the case, but often you will want to create a system before delegating so that you set them up for success. More on this soon.)

And what is left—the items that don't have X, D, or S beside them—are yours to own. That's what you'll keep doing, and these items should either be:

a)   High-value growth-oriented CEO activities
b)   Tasks you love doing and want to keep

The rest you should offload asap—hopefully, freeing up 10 to 25 hours (or more) per week!

Specific Task	Hrs/Week	Tier	Energy	XDS	New Owner
Leading Team Meetings	2.5	3-Manager	↓ Takes My Energy	S+D	Aaron
New Client Setup + Welcome	1.5	1-Admin	↓ Takes My Energy	S	Charine
Weekly Social Media Content	3.0	2-Tech	Neutral	X	- -
Creating Strategic Partnerships	4.5	4-Exec	↑ Gives Me Energy	- -	

And the final step with this process is to go through the remaining items that aren't cut out and put who the owner of that particular item will be. You may need to hire someone to fill that role; if so, write "need to hire" next to it. We need to know who is responsible for each task.

Now, once you complete this exact process, it's time to take a good hard look in the mirror. Where has your time been going, and how does that compare to where you defined your time *should* be going in your top five responsibilities?

Has most of your time gone to high-impact growth activities? Or was it wasted on tasks that a seven-figure CEO shouldn't be doing?

Having all of your tasks mapped out in this way can be a true eye-opener.

One of our clients, Joe, realized that 96% of his tasks could be—and *should* be—offloaded. Nearly everything! He went on to have a record-setting year and much better balance with a newborn child at home after going through this process. And we've had countless others do the same.

Time is the constraint to solve for.

You have plenty of it, but it's how you spend your time that matters most. This is the ultimate leading indicator that tells so much about where you're headed.

So use this simple process as your guide to get clear and focused on what matters most. I have done it every month for years now, and will continue to do so as I always find more tasks to offload.

Block off 30 minutes to work through this. Once you have an inventory of your tasks, it's time to prioritize and remove these off your plate one by one. This order helps:

1. Start with the items to cut (X)
2. Then the things you hate most that zap your energy (☒)
3. Then the admin stuff (Tier 1)
4. Then everything else

Take action here and your life won't ever be the same.

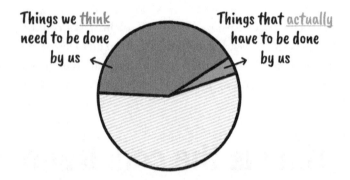

Things we *think* need to be done by us ←

Things that *actually* have to be done → by us

6-Figure Hustler	7-Figure CEO
• Responsible for multiple dozens of tasks each week • Still doing a lot of Admin and Technician work • Busy, but not super effective • Spread too thin and not spending enough time on high-impact activities • Afraid to cut things out, thinking they "have to" do things • Don't have the team to delegate things to	• Clear on the value of their time • Consistently offloading and delegating non-critical tasks • Free from all Admin and Technician day-to-day work • Not afraid to cut things out; knows this is the best form of simplification • Delegates using systems

The Delegation Flow

How cool would it be if you mastered delegation?

Well, let me show you how.

Odds are that you've tried delegating many times before. But if you're like many other business owners, this often ends up:

- Taking *more* time than it'd take you to do it
- Causing more frustration
- Slowing everything else down
- And wasting your hard-earned money

You think, *"I knew I should have just handled it myself."*

So you do, holding onto things you shouldn't be doing for way too long. As a result, you stay stuck on the six-figure hamster wheel overwhelmed and exhausted with an endless to-do list.

That was me for years. I thought nobody could do tasks as fast or as well as me. They would make it worse, and I'd be wasting money every time I tried to delegate. So I held on to these things, and that led to me being burned out so bad that I had to call 911 with a massive anxiety attack. Not once, but twice!

And then I learned a very important lesson:

To get to a highly successful multi-seven-figure machine, you *must* let go and break that cycle. You must delegate. And the key is, you have to delegate the *right* way—not how you've done it in the past.

Here's how delegation typically happens. Tell me if this sounds familiar:

- You get overwhelmed and know you need to delegate...

- So you give it a shot, optimistic that it's going to work. You think, "*This is pretty simple. It's easy.*"
- So you delegate something to your team…
- But it doesn't get done or isn't correct. You need to step in and fix it.
- Now you're behind—and stress kicks in…
- You are in a hurry, frustrated, and just do it yourself, reinforcing those beliefs that your team sucks and that you should have just handled it.

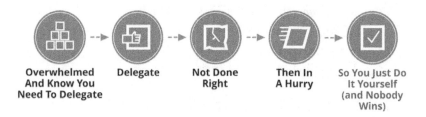

When delegation falls into this pattern, you end up *worse* than when you began! It took time, money, energy, and frustration—all to get the same or worse results. Not good!

But here's the thing: more than 90% of the time, delegation fails because of you, not your team. To flip that around and do it right, you have to follow the 2X Delegation Flow.

The 2X Delegation Flow

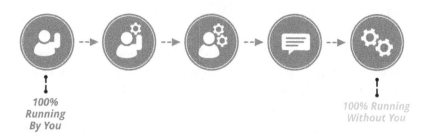

With this process, you'll have much better success in delegating. It'll set your team up to do the task well, and this way, everyone wins. Here are the steps to follow:

Step 1 - Record Your Steps (v1 System)

You are already doing the task you want to offload. So, the first step is to create a system while you do that task.

I'll repeat: you're already doing the work! Now just press record as you do the task, using some simple software on your computer, or jot down the exact steps you walk through piece by piece to create the first version of a process. This will be a blueprint others will follow to complete the task that you're wanting to offload.

Someone else can clean up the process you create and make it perfect; you just need that first iteration, so as you go through this next week start to document your steps on a few simple tasks to offload. It'll take a few extra minutes to create a lot of free brainspace over time...*AND* it'll set your team up for much more clarity on what to do than just giving the task.

Most say they're too busy to create processes/systems, but if you don't do it, then you won't ever effectively delegate—and you'll stay 'too busy' forever! You choose.

Step 2 - Make A Clear Hand-Off

The second step that most never quite work through is a great hand-off. We *think* we communicate the task well, but in reality, not so much.

I know I spent the majority of my first few years in business trying to delegate. The bad thing is, I didn't give nearly enough *or* the right information at all. I wasn't clear and specific. They were supposed to know what I meant and read my mind. Obviously, most times that didn't work out.

Here's what a clear hand-off includes:

Definition of Done (DOD)
What does success for this task look like? What is the end result that you're looking for?

Defining this and listing it out in detail is going to give them a clear idea of exactly what to deliver and complete.

Responsibility
Make sure it's very clear that it is now their responsibility. This may seem obvious, but oftentimes, they aren't really 100% sure that you delegated a new responsibility to them.

Make it super clear that this is now theirs and that you handed it off. One way to do this is to make sure all tasks you delegate off are put into a project management system with the details.

Timing
When is it due? How urgent is this, and how does it fit into their other priorities?

We often think it's clear whether something is urgent, but trust me, unless you communicate it, then most people won't know! So help them.

Share a due date and note whether it's a high-, medium-, or low-priority task. Make this clear so your employee/contractor knows when to get a task delivered.

Also, it's helpful to state how long something should take. Be conservative; if it takes you 10-15 minutes to do and you've been doing it for a year, tell them it shouldn't take more than 30 minutes. This way they won't be spending four hours in the wrong direction when something should take a small fraction of that.

Looking at these three elements, how well, on a scale of 1 to 10, have you been doing on making a clear hand-off?

Odds are it's a low score! (See how it's often *your* fault, not theirs?)

Fix this, and all of a sudden your delegation results and team performance will go through the roof, one task at a time.

Step 3 - Feedback Loops

Now your team can take over the task—but not fully. They don't have your knowledge and experience, so they will need some feedback as they handle the nuances and different scenarios.

Set some milestones, and give them a few points of input so they fully understand the task and process. It's good to have a couple check-ins as they get even a portion of the task/project done so that they don't go too far in the wrong direction.

Once you delegate, be sure to follow up, give them an opportunity to ask questions, and give feedback on how they're doing. This brings it full circle and will have you confident they can handle it without you.

Step 4 - Full Ownership

Now, finally, it's time to fully release that task and *let go*.

Your team is clear on what you want, they've been given feedback, they have the process down, and now it's theirs to own. Make this super clear, and update any documents as needed that show this.

Then, you can rest assured that they are exponentially more likely to succeed with the task you've delegated to them.

Here's the 2X Delegation Flow in full:

You Do	You Create v1 System	Clear Hand-Off (Details & DOD)	They Do, You Give Feedback (Milestones)	They Do & Own System
100% Running By You				100% Running Without You

Do this and you'll be a master of delegation.

Sure, it feels like more work—and it *is* in the short term—but you'll feel the positive effects from this almost instantaneously once it's done.

Effective delegation has a major trickle-up effect on the rest of your business, empowering and optimizing your team, freeing up your time and energy, reducing back and forth and reactivity, allowing you to take things to the next level.

To get to seven figures fast, delegation has to be a major strength. Now you have the exact steps to make that happen.

Let's now look at how to turn your business operations and team into a consistent machine that will thrive without you. The next two chapters are crucial.

6-Figure Hustler	7-Figure CEO
• Delegates quickly and without giving the proper details and direction • Expects others to know what you know • Gets frustrated when they don't get it right the first time • Not very clear on what outcome is • Keeps adding more to other's plates without explaining priority and timing or making trade-offs	• Delegates using systems to fully hand-off responsibility • Over-communicates to make sure they fully understand the task, and gives a clear definition of done • Helps others understand the expected timing of the task, when it's due, and how it fits in relation to other priorities • Works together with team to create culture of systems and building a machine

Chapter 3 Big Ideas

- The tipping point of growth comes when you get free from the weeds and start working "on" your business, not being stuck "in" it.

- Give up the superhero cape and thinking that you can do it all, and get into your true role as CEO.

- Define the top role responsibilities you will own and spend 80%+ of your time there.

- Start creating a culture of turning your business into a machine that can thrive without you (or any one key person).

- Leverage one of the best things you can do for your team, time, and growth potential...and *simplify* what isn't essential or making a substantial impact. Cutting things out is the fastest path to free up time.

- XDS™ to cut, delegate and systemize all of the tasks you can to free up at least 10-20 hours per week.

- Create a simple org chart that maps out what your 7-figure business looks like. Then fill in the key six roles one by one, firing yourself and owning a max of two roles (one being CEO).

- Take the extra time to delegate with systems and clarity. Use the 2X Delegation Flow to master delegation once and for all, empowering your team and firing yourself one task at a time... for good.

CHAPTER 4

OPERATIONAL
MACHINE

The Key To Everything You Want

Here's a simple fact:

You can't scale what's broken.

Sounds pretty clear, right? Yet nearly every business owner who comes to us *thinks* they're ready to go straight toward growth. When in fact, 100% of the time, we identify multiple *very* **important items that need to be addressed** *before* **they can scale to the next level.** This is even true of businesses that come to us with seven- or eight-figure revenue already.

When entrepreneurs ignore our advice and try to scale right away, they end up like most businesses:

- Creating more headaches, fires and longer task lists
- Stressing out their team *even* more
- Wasting hard-earned profits on marketing agencies or advertising
- Chasing new idea after new idea, wondering why it's not working

They have the potential and work their butts off only to find themselves with minimal progress. That is a frustrating place to be!

I know because I did that for years.

The good news is, growing a wildly successful business doesn't have to be that way—if you get the key elements right.

At 2X, we spend weeks with clients (already six- or seven-figure businesses) to build and optimize their foundation. That's what we've been talking about so far—the strategy, Model ONE™, understanding and targeting your ideal audience in detail, making offers irresistible, freeing up time, etc.—the pieces you need to prepare to scale your business.

Once those are cleaned up, *then* we can start to talk about growth and drive some incredible results. But there's one more piece you need.

The growth doesn't matter if you can't handle it or it's not consistent. What you want is predictable, controlled growth. To do that, where we don't have the big peaks and valleys and you're growing consistently, we need to turn your business into an *operational machine*.

The key to everything you want—freedom, growth, income, impact, and long-term success… is to turn your business into a *machine*!

By focusing on the foundation first, and then turning your business into a machine, you can have repeatable, sustainable growth for years.

Plus, you can do so while working less! That's the dream—and is a reality if you follow our 2X methodology.

Now, this talk of an operational machine may not be as 'sexy' as talking about the latest marketing hacks to do, but trust me: it is way more powerful than almost anything else.

So that's what this chapter is all about.

Your New Best Friend

Dogs are pretty damn special, but they may need to move to second place. Let me introduce you to your new best friend as a business owner:

Systems.

Systems set you free. They're the key to scaling with consistency and control.

They're the key to speed, delegation, exponentially growing your team output, and much more!

They're the center of your business machine, and they are the secret weapon I hope you, after reading this, *never* run your business without again.

Two Ways To Run Your Business	
With Systems	**Without Systems**
• Consistency	• *Hustle & Muscle*
• Control	• Reactivity
• Set Team Up For Success	• Inconsistency
• Delegate	• Reliant On You
• Time Freedom!	• Trading Time For Money
• Efficiency	• Chaos & Overwhelm
• Growth	• Unpredictable Revenue

Even before this chapter, you knew you needed systems, but *what does that even mean?*

And where do you start? It's amazing how many business owners don't really even know what systems are or how to use them, so they never do.

Just in case that hits a little close to home, let's start with the basics.

A system is a method of solving a task in a strategic, repeatable, and efficient way.

Now, this can come in many forms. Here are the main seven types:

1. Checklist
2. SOP: standard operating procedure (step-by-step process)
3. Software application or tech tool
4. Video process
5. Automation
6. Template
7. Combination

A system can be big or small—from a simple individual process to a collection of processes and systems all together, such as a comprehensive hiring system or sales system that includes a number of elements.

Here are a few examples of different systems:

- Sales script
- Handling payroll
- Quarterly planning
- New client onboarding
- Writing effective blog posts
- Setting up blog articles on your site
- Employee monthly performance reviews

The thing is…

Everything you do in business should be a system!

Everything.

It sounds a bit overwhelming, but it's not. The fact is, **you're already doing more than enough work!** You're already putting in more than enough hours. We just need to turn that work into systems that can make things easier, faster, and repeatable—so that you can get into a true CEO role.

This allows you and your team to get a lot more done with a lot more consistency a lot more easily. I cannot overstate their importance. It's a huge difference between multiple six-figures and overworked…and being at multiple seven-figures with a business that works *for* you.

Now, don't get overwhelmed here. This is where most entrepreneurs shut down and think they'll start creating systems in a month or two. You don't have to create hundreds of systems for your company. And definitely not in one week. Just like with anything, get the 80/20 right and you'll be set up to win big.

Here are some of the 80/20 systems you'll need to get to seven figures fast:

1. **Hiring System:** to recruit and hire great people
2. **Numbers/Data Systems:** to have clarity, drive decision-making, and accountability
3. **Planning Systems:** to help you and your team take the 'simplest, most direct path' with a clear, strategic plan each week/month/quarter
4. **Employee Management and Review Systems:** to help optimize and improve your team every month
5. **Financial Systems:** to make sure cash is a source of fuel for your business, not holding you back
6. **Marketing Systems:** to drive consistent, repeatable growth, not just peaks and valleys
7. **Sales System:** to effectively convert leads into customers
8. **Onboarding and Fulfillment Systems:** to keep you out of the 'weeds' and repeatedly turn customers into raving fans

Get these right, and you'll be off to the races like never before. For templates and a free deep-dive training on this, check out your 7-Figure Toolkit at 2X.co/toolkit.

Systems are something few entrepreneurs truly adopt, but if and when you do, you'll join the top 4%, for sure.

6-Figure Hustler	7-Figure CEO
• "Too busy" to create systems • Not clear on exactly what systems are or how to leverage them to scale better/faster • Doesn't train their team on systems either, thus always fighting fires	• Learns to love and leverage systems • Understands that everything can (and *should*) be a system • Crafts a culture where the team creates, improves, and uses systems regularly • Maps out and creates the key 80/20 high impact systems needed • Team is creating systems as they do the work, to set up for more efficiency in the future

What Your Machine Looks Like

After graduation, I moved straight south from the cold weather of small-town Ohio to the big, hot, and muggy city of Houston, Texas, to work for a massive oil company.

I started out as a shy, reserved, introverted engineer. On day two, the 'big boss' of our division walks up to me. He was an intimidating man, especially for a new person like me. He doesn't say anything at all, just looks at me and waves his finger to follow him.

My heart stops. I shuffle around, grab a notebook, and follow him into the executive boardroom. I'm scared as hell as he gets near the whiteboard and starts talking.

"Austin, do you know why we're so successful?" he asks.

I have no clue and can't spit out any words at all, so I just shake my head.

He proceeds to map out each key step for our entire business step by step, from the crude oil process to the packaged end-product we sold to our customers.

> *"We're so successful because what we do is break up every part of our business, and treat each step as its own entire business. When each step is optimized, performing, and profitable, then it adds up to something pretty special."*

I didn't think too much of it at the time. I was just trying to comprehend what he was saying, but it made sense. He was mapping out our complex business into a few simple high-level steps so that he could see the 30,000-foot view at all times.

He didn't need to be in the nuances of the day-to-day. He didn't need to be in the trenches. He could see the big picture. This allowed him and the other executives to easily identify what was working, what wasn't, where to focus and what to fix. At any given time, they could see the primary bottleneck holding things back.

Plus, by treating every micro-step as its own business that could be optimized independently, it added up to a highly profitable, well-performing business *machine*!

This top-down view forever changed the way I saw business, and it's now at the center of our 2X *Machine Methodology*.

We call this framework the Value Chain. For each business we work with, we map out the key steps in their business, from someone not knowing them at all, all the way through being a raving fan. This could be five to seven steps, but let's keep it really simple to start.

Here's your business:

The three high-level steps in your business are marketing, sales and fulfillment. Marketing's goal is to generate qualified leads. Sales' goal is to generate customers from those leads. And Fufillment's goals are to create raving fan customers for life (CFLs).

With this high-level view and the key metrics for each phase, you can identify exactly where the bottleneck is and focus on that. This is game-changing because…

The more clearly you understand the specific problem, the easier it is to solve that problem.

So instead of trying to fix your entire business at once, let's break it down into much smaller chunks and focus on ONE at a time. This will save you time and effort, and drive a lot more results.

Plus, the key of everything that I'm sharing in this book is to make sure that we not only drive growth, but that we do so with you being free from the weeds and that we drive consistent, predictable growth. The way that we do that is by turning your business into a *MACHINE*.

To do so, we need to take this Value Chain methodology and have each specific phase be able to thrive without you. To make that happen, there are four key elements for each step.

1 - Strategy

Do you have the right strategy and plan of attack for each step?

Can you make it simpler or more strategic to drive the desired result?

Let's say that you want to double your leads. Remember the Million Dollar Question, *"What's the simplest and most direct path to achieve that result?"*

Getting strategic and intentional to make sure you have the right strategy for each phase to achieve your goals is the key starting spot. From there you can see exactly what you need for the next three elements.

2 - Owner+Team

At the beginning, you probably own marketing, sales, *AND* fulfillment. But to scale to multiple millions, that cannot happen. So, one by one, we need to get you free from the day-to-day and ideally only in the CEO role.

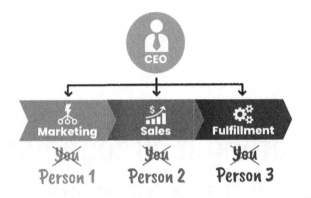

For now, it's okay to own one or two elements as you scale and generate more cash flow to replace you, but this will be a major focus. Identify which key role you'll fully remove yourself from first.

Now, for each phase, the department owner is also responsible for making sure they have the proper team and resources to get the results. Just don't start here. Start with a clear, simple and effective strategy (remember the MDQ) before building your team.

3 - Numbers

What are the metrics that matter most for each step? What are the conservative targets of where you need to be to hit your goals, and where are you at now? List those out so you can see which parts of your business are strong or weak. These will be your guide to tell you what's working, what's not, where to focus and what to fix.

These are essential and most entrepreneurs struggle immensely to track and manage the right metrics. Start small and build up with just a couple key metrics for each phase.

4 - Systems

As you know, systems are your secret weapon. They drive consistency, repeatability and scalability. You don't need a thousand systems, but a few key systems for each step will be revolutionary for your business and team. List out the top three to five systems per stage that will drive more consistency, performance, and time to work on even higher impact activities.

Putting it all together, you'll have a consistent, predictable, cash-producing *machine*.

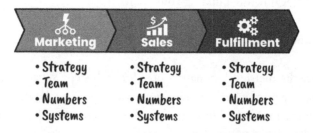

The owner of each step should always have a plan to guide and own each of these elements. As soon as you do, your business will be on the fast-track to the next level.

Now, the cool thing is that this methodology of the Value Chain and turning your business into a machine isn't just to reach $1M per year. This is the same approach we use with all of our seven and eight-figure clients we've worked with, as well—and are a key to our results.

Plus, my same mentor who taught me this went on to become the CEO of a $6 billion pipeline company. So, long story short, this methodology flat-out works no matter who you are or what level you're at. And it'll work for you!

6-Figure Hustler	7-Figure CEO
• Tries to fix your business as a whole • Unable to see exactly what the real bottleneck is, so is often fixing the wrong problem • Strategy is too complex or not optimal for each specific step of your Value Chain	• Able to see business from a 30,000 foot view perspective to identify the overall business health and key bottleneck • Breaks down the business into distinct micro steps to be able to drive consistency and improvements with more focus • Has a clear, strategic, intentional and simple *strategy* for each major phase • Uses systems, numbers, and a team to make each step be a consistent, repeatable machine

Where Growth Begins

If you ask almost any six-figure entrepreneur how to double their business as fast as possible, they'll probably start telling you about marketing tactics and ideas.

What if I told you it's better to save marketing for last?

Since working with entrepreneurs from different industries and all over the world—and helping our clients grow by over $255 million in the last three years—I've learned that...

Growth actually begins in fulfillment.

Done right, improving fulfillment makes everything else easier and possible. This little secret resolves many of the issues six-figure businesses face. When you create best-in-class fulfillment, you:

1. Make raving fan clients.
2. Raving fan clients buy more from you.
3. They tell their friends and share about you (your best form of marketing).
4. Those happy clients (and their referrals) are easier and better to work with, and become more successful more often.
5. You get out of the weeds and don't get pulled in to fix issues all of the time, so you can continue to focus on growth.
6. You can also handle more clients as you grow.

7. Your team is less stressed and making a bigger impact.
8. Your profitability goes through the roof.
9. Your average client LTV rises, so you can reinvest more back into the business.

And more!

It's this crazy compound effect that all starts with **world-class fulfillment!**

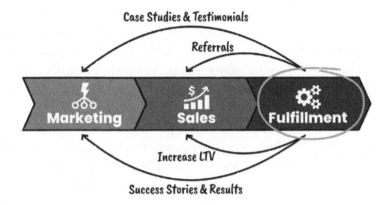

Most entrepreneurs think that their products are great. *But are you making truly raving fans? Are they sending you referrals left and right?* If not, you have an opportunity to improve your fulfillment.

Done right, great fulfillment creates this 'organic viral loop'—driving more leads and repeat business, more consistently, and on autopilot. It's the best form of marketing you can have!

This one variable that most ignore brings an exponential impact across everything you do. You create a much healthier, stronger, more sustainable and scalable business, a happier team, and way less stress.

To have strong, *scalable* fulfillment, you'll want to have three key pieces in line.

1 - Internal Operations

Do you have the actions listed out step-by-step for how to deliver your product effectively and make raving fans?

Get this mapped out in detail to drive more consistency, repeatability, and make your fulfillment be ready to handle a lot more customers.

2 - Internal Hiring & Fulfillment Training

What so many small businesses do is have their business dependent on one person. If somebody quits, it throws the company for a loop. You want to be ready to replace every role, especially fulfillment as this is most likely a role you'll hire for numerous times in the future.

So, not only do you want to be ready to recruit and fill your key fulfillment roles. But more importantly, you want to have a structured onboarding to get new hires up to speed and performing so that it doesn't take a ton of time from you each time you need to fill those roles!

If you do this, your fulfillment is then ready to scale and you can sleep like a baby knowing that you won't keep getting pulled back into client delivery.

3 - Client-Facing Systems

And of course, you need the client-facing systems and assets to make for a great experience too.

If you have all three of these in place and effective, your fulfillment is very much scalable, repeatable, and not dependent on any one person.

This is what one of our private clients, Jordan Gill, did in the 2X Accelerator to help take her time and business to the next level. Right near the time of joining 2X, she had one of her key coaches quit. This threw her into a stressful situation where she had to jump back into fulfillment with clients as she worked overtime to hire and train the replacement. She was already stressed out before the coach quit, so this put her over the edge.

But fast-forward a few months, and she not only got back out of fulfillment, she put each of these three elements in place to be set up to hire and train more coaches in the future. As a result, she took her business from $436k per year (and mostly stuck in the weeds!)...to 3X'ing her revenue to over $1.2 million while also being almost *completely* removed from all of her day-to-day operations!

Plus, she now has the infrastructure to keep going up and up, with scalable fulfillment. This is priceless peace of mind!

So if you want to scale like this too, listen to this:

Big, consistent growth starts with world-class fulfillment.

Odds are that you're good at what you do. But I challenge you to make this a focus and take the next step. If you become truly world-class at what you do and combine that with a few other growth levers I'm sharing in this book, you'll dominate any and every niche you go into.

Get this wrong, and you'll be constantly muscling growth. Get this right and anything is possible. You choose.

6-Figure Hustler	7-Figure CEO
• Thinks they "just need more leads" as the key to their growth • Doesn't have scalable fulfillment • Isn't producing raving fan customers • Has a wide range of mixed client results • Keeps getting pulled back into fulfillment to fix issues or help with clients	• Understands that raving fans are at the heart of great business and that growth begins with fulfillment • Has scalable, repeatable fulfillment *without* them involved • Strong, repeatable fulfillment making raving fans who drive strong LTV and referrals

How To Make Easier, Faster, Better Decisions

Want to make easier, faster, better decisions? Here's your secret weapon.

It's something that over 95% of the entrepreneurs we've worked with don't do well at.

It's knowing your key numbers inside and out.

Numbers are fact. They are reality. They don't care about stories or excuses. They tell you exactly what's going on: what's working, what's not, where to focus and what to fix.

In business, *numbers rule.*

They are your guide to the next level.

When we come into a company or start working with a business, the first thing we ask after the vision and goals is, *what are the numbers?*

Ninety-nine percent don't know them! They think they know some of the key metrics or financials, but when we look into it, they are often significantly off. And if you don't know the numbers, you can't make objective decisions.

I can't emphasize this enough. Numbers are at the center of your multi-million dollar business machine. If you want to make your job easier and start making better, faster decisions, let the numbers be your secret weapon.

At 2X, we track a lot of numbers to pinpoint the problems and opportunities to address. But you don't need to start there. There are two primary ways to think about your numbers:

Part 1: Your Success Formula

Your business is a formula. What we need to do is map out the key metrics that matter, and then identify where you're at now, and what the best levers are to get you to your goals.

Let's use your simple 3-step Value Chain as the guide here.

First, what you want to identify are what are the most important metrics to track for each phase of your business.

For marketing, maybe your top metric is the number of qualified applications per month. For sales, it could then be your close ratio of those qualified applications. And for fulfillment, it could be customer lifetime value (LTV). So, the start of your success formula would look like this:

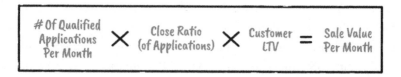

Then what we'd want to do is start to track what those actual numbers are right now.

	Marketing	Sales	Fulfillment	
KPI:	Applications Per Month	Close Ratio (of Applications)	LTV	Sale Value
Current:	24	18%	$8,000	$34.5k/mo

And then lastly, let's think about each step strategically. Remember the first of four pieces of your cash-producing machine? It's the right strategy for each phase of your Value Chain.

If you get really intentional and focus on driving the key metrics for each phase one by one, where do you think you could get them to in the next 6 months? Let's set your targets to achieve for each step.

	Marketing	Sales	Fulfillment	
KPI:	Applications Per Month	Close Ratio (of Applications)	LTV	Sale Value
Current:	24	18%	$8,000	$34.5k/mo
Target:	36	22%	$11,000	$87k/mo

This will be your success formula. This is what you're working towards.

Then from here, you'll be able to track your progress for each metric. Everyone on your team can be clear on what metric to drive, and you can see the impact. **Even modest improvements compounded lead to some massive results.**

In this above example, with fairly small improvements for marketing, sales, and fulfillment, the business 2.5X'ed their sale value. Plus, they are above the magic $1 million per year rate of $83,333 per month.

This is the power of the machine and Value Chain done right. This approach is priceless.

Part 2: The Top 10 Numbers

The second way to master your numbers is by identifying the top ~10 metrics that drive your business. If you do this, you'll be well ahead of 95% of entrepreneurs and have more clarity than ever of where to focus.

Those 10 metrics may not be immediately obvious, and they are often different for every business. Sure, some will be similar (e.g. revenue and profit), but you need to figure out what the most important numbers are for *your* business. Ask yourself:

> *If I had to make all of my business decisions based on only 10 numbers, what would they be?*

You'll likely want some KPIs (key performance indicators) related to:

- Profit
- Cash
- Client Satisfaction
- Customer Lifetime Value (LTV)
- Cost to Acquire New Customers (CAC)
- Employee Satisfaction/Performance
- A Leading Marketing Metric (e.g. number of qualified leads)
- Number of Sales Opportunities (e.g. sales calls scheduled)
- Sales Conversions

Spend some time identifying the 10 most important metrics for your business, and take a deeper dive into KPIs with templates and examples in your 7-Figure Toolkit (2X.co/toolkit).

To show you a specific example, the top 10 metrics we track at 2X are:

1. Revenue Growth (total rolling 90-day revenue chart)
2. Average Customer Lifetime Value (LTV)
3. Churn Rate (how many clients cancel; you could also do client success rate or customer satisfaction, such as Net Promoter Score, but we like churn as a top metric to know)
4. Cost to Acquire Customer (CAC, broken down by channel and overall)
5. Monthly Free Cash Flow (you could track profit margin)
6. Number of Sales Opportunities (booked sales calls, only counting those who are qualified)
7. Close Ratio (of total qualified sales opportunities)
8. Core Capital (making sure we are ahead financially; more on this soon)
9. Employee NPS
10. And a leading metric for our top marketing focus at the moment

If I know these, I'll know at least 90% of the story of what's going on in the business. From there, we can then understand where our time and energy need to go.

If you don't know the top numbers that drive your business yet, block off some time this week to figure them out. It may be painful to go through at first. You may not be a "numbers person."

But if you drive your business without knowing these, it's the equivalent of driving your car blindfolded. You will not get where you want to go, and you will crash a lot on the way there!

Now, one other thing to note. The first time you dive into the numbers, they may be more depressing than you thought. But having this view will give you the power of clarity that can then lead you to make much better decisions moving forward.

One of our clients has had a 'successful' multi-million dollar business as a well-known market leader in his niche, working with celebrities. The bad thing is, prior to 2X, he didn't know his numbers at all.

When we dove in, we realized that most of his business was not profitable! He wasn't pricing himself the right way, so a lot of his high-end projects were not only stressing him out, they were literally *losing* him money. This put him on this seemingly never-ending financial hamster wheel. Without knowing the numbers and his finances, he was positioned to *be stuck* working and chasing money forever!

But then getting clear on the metrics wasn't easy at first. He said, *"I didn't sleep well for a month, but now I know my damn numbers!"* Now he has a great plan of action on what to do (and what to stop doing), and has been profitable and growing, even during what is typically his 'dead' season!

I cannot reiterate how important knowing and acting on your top metrics are.

You can either guess and hustle *or* make easier, better, faster decisions using the numbers as your guide.

You'll join the elite business owners when you do.

6-Figure Hustler	7-Figure CEO
• "Too busy" to track the key metrics • Doesn't know what the top metrics to track are • For the numbers they do track, they aren't consistent or 100% accurate • Team also isn't clear on key numbers and isn't held accountable to them • Not sure exactly what real issue is, oftentimes fixing the wrong problem due to lack of clarity	• Key metrics clearly defined and tracked regularly • Has a "success formula" of what key metrics to hit for each step of the Value Chain • Use numbers in all meetings and each week to drive decision making • Team is fully aware of key metrics and using them to guide team performance and accountability • Able to see exactly where key issues and opportunities are • Using the numbers to drive more consistency and growth ongoing

Cash Flow Or Die

Speaking of numbers, the stats are not encouraging.

- More than half of businesses fail in the first five years.
- Only 40% are profitable, while 30% are continually *losing* money![3]
- And 96% never make it past $1 million!

But do you know the biggest 'official' reason why businesses fail?

They run out of cash. One study showed that 82% of companies that fail do so due to cashflow problems.[4]

Cash is the oxygen and life-blood of your business. It's not only what keeps the lights on, but also what can fuel the explosion…*and* of course that lifestyle you're after, too!

Here are a few principles for making sure you have the cash you need to fuel it all:

1 - Stop Mixing

When you're starting out, it's easy to mix your business and personal finances, but as you're graduating from 'hustle' to *real* business, it's time to go pro.

Go Pro In Your Business

[3]   Wallace, David. "Infographic: The Most Tried And Failed Small Businesses." *Small Business Trends,* 15 March 2013, https://smallbiztrends.com/2013/03/infographic-failed-small-businesses.html

[4]   Berry, Tim. "10 Critical Cash Flow Rules." *Entrepreneur, 30 November 2007,* https://www.entrepreneur.com/article/187366

Stop treating your business as a piggy bank and get things separated. Sure, this may add a few more dollars in taxes short-term, but it'll keep you out of trouble and making better decisions for your business.

So, take a few minutes, set up different accounts, and fully separate your personal and business accounts and credit cards like a real business owner would.

2 - Get A Bookkeeper & Rhythm

Get a bookkeeper and make sure your main financial reports are updated regularly. At the least, get them updated and reconciled each month.

Then, the main part of this is…actually learn what your financial reports (primarily your Profit & Loss or Income Statement) are telling you. Spend the time to review this every month as soon as it's sent to you, and each time identify 2-3 key levers to focus on improving your top and bottom lines.

3 - Core Capital

Core capital is the amount of money you have in your business account versus your upcoming expenses.

If your average monthly expenses are $40,000 and you have $40,000 in the business bank account in cash, then you have one month of core capital. If you have only $20,000 in cash, you have only two weeks of runway! That's a scary spot to be.

Two months of cash is the *minimum* suggested amount.

This way, if no new sales come in at all, you can rest assured that you don't have to make week-to-week survival decisions and can keep focused on the *right* actions. This puts you at ease and in the power position.

Work to get ahead financially…and stay there!

4 - Be On Top Of A/R

If business owners just got what they were owed on time, then most cash flow issues wouldn't exist!

Make sure you track your outstanding A/R (accounts receivable, which is money owed to you). And definitely make sure you have the systems in place to get what you're owed on time. The longer you wait, the harder it is to actually receive that money so stay on top of this.

It's not uncommon for us to see companies owed more than $50,000 in past-due invoices! It's crazy. Put an end to that once and for all, no matter how big or small your open A/R is.

5 - Set Targets

And lastly, set targets for each key financial metric, including each main line item of your P&L. If you review your numbers each month and take a couple key actions every month, you will have more confidence, clarity and control of your finances. And you will drive more profitability than ever before.

So, start to make forecasts each month and track how you do compared to these. Over time, you'll get more accurate and make better decisions to drive your business to that big vision of yours.

Most entrepreneurs never take this seriously, and stay on the cash flow rollercoaster for years. But start with these five tips, and you'll be on the fast-track to millions with a cash-producing machine.

6-Figure Hustler	7-Figure CEO
• Not very profitable • Always seems to be at-risk and/or behind with finances, never quite getting ahead for good • Doesn't understand profitability of various products or marketing channels • No forecast or targets set • Doesn't fully understand key financial statements in detail • No A/R systems in place, and regularly gets behind with money owed to you	• Has more than two months of expenses saved in the bank as a baseline • Clear on your financials • Strong profitability and cash flow • Understands margins by product and by key marketing channel • Regularly reviews financials…and takes actions each month to continually improve • A/R systems in place and on top of money owed

Go To The Source

Though I've tried to show you the value of offloading your responsibilities, sometimes you have to take things into your own hands. But when that happens, don't just fix the thing and move on—go to the source!

This mentality is what Howard Schultz, former CEO of Starbucks, has used to help build one of the top companies in the world. My favorite story about him goes as follows:

Mr. Schultz was on a trip and went to one of many Starbucks locations. At the store, a light in the sign was out. This was not a good look for the manager there, as Schultz was making a very rare one-time visit.

What could Howard have done here?

A. Have the staff fix it right away
B. Get mad and reprimand the store manager
C. Neither of the above

(He chose C.)

What he did instead is a crucial reason why Starbucks has such an insanely successful and scalable business.

Per the story, Howard immediately called back to headquarters and asked:

"What is our process to handle a light being out?"

He could have handled it a bunch of different ways, but he immediately went to the *source* of the problem. He addressed the **system** so that this problem wouldn't happen again.

He didn't immediately go to the Band-Aid solution to fix that single bulb. He focused on the big lever (the system) that would impact his entire chain of stores.

That mentality and thinking is absolutely game-changing.

Any issue comes up? Don't get frustrated. Don't yell. Try not to even fix the issue right away.

Instead, go to the source and fix the system! Create this as a mentality for yourself and as part of your company culture.

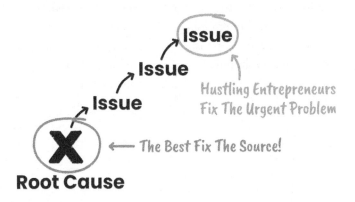

Go to the SOURCE and fix the SYSTEM!

Imagine, if every issue is solved with a system improvement, what would that mean for your growth and success? I'll tell you: it'd mean more freedom, consistency, growth, and a business machine that is working *for* you, not the other way around.

I know, as a busy entrepreneur, it's hard to transform your business into a systemized company, but making the shift to fixing every problem with systems is absolutely essential if you want to have the success that you and I know is possible.

Lead your team to turn your business into a machine, one system at a time, and you can start to take over your market like Howard has.

6-Figure Hustler	7-Figure CEO
• Keep putting fire after fire out, without going to what is really causing the fires • Has team trained to do tasks, without a focus on systems and long-term solutions	• Identifies the root cause of problems and addresses that • Fix every problem with a system so that it doesn't become a problem again • Create a culture of using systems to reduce errors and problems

0% Reactivity

There's a tendency to make business way more complicated and stressful than it needs to be. One of the keys of self-induced stress in a business is what the majority of entrepreneurs are all too familiar with: reactivity.

When there's reactivity:

- You get stressed and angry
- Your team gets stressed
- Everyone gets rushed
- Bad decisions are made
- The quality drops

And nobody wins.

Reactivity can cripple a business, and unfortunately, most are running their businesses like a constant train on fire with no end in sight!

The good news is, it doesn't have to be that way. You can scale fast and not have the stress. You can have things be ahead, calm, and focused—if you master the principle of **0% Reactivity.**

This means removing the need to react from your day-to-day operations where no actions are needed that same day. This is a lofty goal to live up to, but it's more than possible.

We've implemented this into our culture, and it's been game-changing. The compound effect this makes is:

- Way less stress
- Better decision-making
- Less turnover and burnout
- Happier employees and stronger culture

- More productivity and efficiency
- More of working on the *right* activities

You can do the same and get to 0% Reactivity with these two tips:

1 - The 72-Hour Rule

In our business, nothing should ever be needed that same day. Nothing.

Everything should be done, ready, and approved ahead of time. So everyone can plan their day and do as much deep, uninterrupted work as possible.

We have a '72-hour rule' that if you need something from someone else, you should request it at a minimum 72 hours ahead of time.

Every person on your team (not just you) has some important things to get done, and if you pull them off their work to be reactive, **that has a major ripple effect**. Then you wonder why they aren't getting anything important done?

Rushed work doesn't convert. It doesn't help you get more done, and it sure doesn't age well in the marathon that is entrepreneurship.

Implement some type of rule that people can't request urgent deadlines. Maybe it's 24 hours to start, but we like the 72-hour request rule.

It's easy to get addicted to the *busyness* of business. But put an end to that.

Slow things down, get ahead, and you'll notice it instantly.

2 - The 0% Reactivity Log

By making things tangible, it's much easier to address. So, we created a spreadsheet log to list out any reactivity that comes up in our day-to-day operations.

Each time it does, we go to the source to analyze how it happened and plan out what systems we need to create/improve to make sure it doesn't happen again.

Here's an example:

Department	Issue	Reason	System Fixes
Marketing	Webinar wasn't ready to launch in time; loss of potential QL's	- Missed content deadline; caused other delays - Not enough review time pre-launch	- More advanced notice of webinars (4 weeks) - Streamline and update content review process; add 7 day buffer

Create your own reactivity sheet (from your 7-Figure Toolkit at 2X.co/toolkit) and make it a habit for your team to analyze why these issues happen.

Every problem is a system opportunity.

So track each fire, analyze it, and address it with a system. The result is a bigger, better, less stressful business.

Make this change starting today, and it begins with *you*. No more reactivity.

6-Figure Hustler	7-Figure CEO
• Too busy to focus on anything but the short-term actions...so stays stuck on the six-figure hamster wheel • Unknowingly creates a culture of reactivity, adding stress and reducing productivity of everyone • Not ahead on tasks with clear plan of action	• Creates a culture of 0% Reactivity so that everyone can do deep work and not be reacting to fires • Slows down to speed up, really analyzing problems and the resulting best solution for the long-term • Addresses problems with systems to reduce problems and errors in the future

Get Your Team Humming!

You want your company pulsing and moving with an energy and momentum where the team is on fire, everyone's clear, and you're moving fast as a unit.

For that, you need the right meeting structure and cadence.

Most six-figure entrepreneurs have no set meetings or rhythm. If they do, they're often inconsistent and a waste of everyone's time (and your hard-earned money!).

We have to change that.

A good meeting rhythm and structure limits reactivity, improves communication, gets everyone aligned, improves the culture, and helps everyone move more efficiently.

Here are the top six meetings and time-blocks that need to go on your calendar immediately.

1 - The Daily Huddle

This is the 80/20 of meetings that we broke down in detail in Chapter 5. If you do only five actions from this book, make this one of them.

It's a very short meeting every workday with your entire team (or department if it's more than ~8 people) to improve communication and management with one central daily check-in. This way, everyone brings their main updates here, dramatically reducing the back-and-forth throughout the day that often pulls people (and most importantly you) away from tasks and out of focus.

Train your team to stop the reactivity throughout the day and bring their questions and challenges to the Daily Huddle…and watch your company's output double with one move.

2 - Weekly Planning

At the beginning of the week, make sure everyone is clear on the best, simplest path forward and the key tasks to get accomplished. A great week starts with a great plan.

What we recommend here is getting every individual clear on their Big 3: the three highest priority actions that they commit to getting done. Three important things per week means you will make meaningful progress each and every week.

3 - Weekly Review

Reflect, learn, and problem-solve to make next week even better so you iterate and improve each and every week. Do this as a team—and also by yourself as the leader—and you'll become unstoppable in no time!

It doesn't take long, but goes a long way if you reflect and learn each week. Plus, you have to drive a culture of accountability, so take a few minutes to make sure that everyone made good progress towards what they said they would. This simple lever of accountability will help you potentially double the output of your team! Yet most small businesses do a horrible job here.

4 - Thinking Time

The CEO's best use of time is making sure the *right* strategy is being followed. Thinking time is a one-hour meeting by yourself to address one big question or challenge.

The best entrepreneurs THINK.

This allows you to stop the chaos, go deep into problem-solving mode, and think critically about your strategy. This is a powerful tool, and will save countless hours by having a better strategy.

Stop the busyness and hustle…and think. Simplify. Get clear and focused on what matters most. This weekly meeting with yourself will help immensely, trust me.

5 - Financials

Not many things are more stressful than finances in a small business. So, to make the leap to 7-figures and do so without the stress, get control of your money. It's time to go pro.

Each week do a quick cash review, going through the key metrics to make sure that you're clear and ahead financially. This will get you out of the week-to-week survival mode and into the *power position*.

You'll be making better decisions and sleeping like a baby at night. That's where you want to be!

6 - Done By 10:30AM™

The key to a great day, great week, great month…is to start fast.

And what we want to do is to have you move your business forward every single day.

To do so, you have to win the morning. One of the best and easiest ways to do that is block off at least two hours every morning for uninterrupted deep work on your most important activities.

We call this our Done By 10:30AM™ system.

The goal is to work on the most important things that will move your business forward *first,* before you get into the fires and reactivity. By 10:30AM, your day should be a massive success.

It's not about busywork. It's about the right activities, so before you enter the blur of the day-to-day, be in control of your time, and work on the million-dollar moves.

Our proven Done By 10:30AM™ system is the best productivity hack out there (in my humble opinion), and you should get your team doing it as well. Learn about the full system in your 7-Figure Toolkit at 2X.co/toolkit.

With the right flow of these six meetings each week, you and your team will feel a new energy and momentum in your business where everyone is more clear and aligned than ever. That's how you can become unstoppable, so get it set up now.

6-Figure Hustler	7-Figure CEO
• Have an inconsistent meeting schedule • Meetings don't have set, effective agendas • No accountability on past actions and commitments • No clear actions or next steps taken from meetings to ensure they get done • Meetings are often waste of people's time • Meetings are one-sided, and not valuable problem solving meetings	• Consistent, simple meeting cadence defined so the team can get into full flow • Meetings have agendas and are valuable time spent • Everyone brings their questions/needs to the meetings instead of having reactivity constantly outside of meetings • Team leaves meetings with clear, recorded actions they are held accountable for • Leveraging thinking time and deep work to get a lot more strategic and bigger results

Chapter 4 Big Ideas

- The key to everything you want—freedom, growth, income, impact, and long-term success…is to turn your business into a *machine*!
- Your business machine consists of the right strategy combined with systems, numbers and your team.
  - o Systems are the key to consistency, repeatability, scalability and getting free from the weeds. Everything in your business is (and should be) a system.
  - o The numbers are your guide. They tell you what's working, what's not, where to focus and what to fix, and will help you make better/faster decisions.
  - o And these two things come before your team…because with the clarity of the numbers and defining what success is along with using systems to make things much more clear, consistent, and repeatable, you set your team up for success.
  - o So again, there is a very important <u>order</u> to things. And getting the operational machine is your *real* money maker that few entrepreneurs learn and leverage.
- The way to run your business is with the Value Chain series of steps to see the top down, high-level view, identify the bottleneck, and build consistency one key phase at a time. Keep it simple to start, then you can break it down into more detail over time by department.
- Have a *Success Formula* that defines the key metrics by phase to hit. Done right, your growth compounds to big numbers with modest improvements.
- Growth begins with fulfillment. Make sure you have the strategy, systems and execution to turn customers into raving fan CFLs (customers for life) at scale—without your time.
- Every problem is a system opportunity. Fix things at the *source* with a system, and you'll continually have less and less fires while improving team performance exponentially.

- Make sure you're clear on your finances and producing cash flow. Then, put the systems in place and work hard to get ahead and into the *power position*. Otherwise, you'll have way more stress and short-term decision making.
- Craft your culture to have *0% Reactivity*; this will reduce stress and increase productivity for everyone!
- Get your team humming with the right cadence and flow of meetings. Done right, this reduces reactivity and increases deep work time for all of your team. Make this happen ASAP!

WORLD-CLASS TEAM

Your Job As CEO

I asked a mentor who had built a $100 million consultancy company, *"What is the key to scale to $10 million and then $100 million?"*

I couldn't even finish my question before he said, *"People!"*

He went on to explain that no matter what level of business you're at...

The most important job of a CEO is to hire great people.

It's an essential key that differentiates fast-scaling businesses from the rest.

This mirrors the advice in Geoff Smart and Randy Street's best-selling book, *Who*. In a survey interviewing approximately 300 top CEOs (including 20-plus billionaires) about what it takes to build a successful business, 52% said the single biggest success factor is management talent.

Not tools. Not products. Not marketing or sales. Not even execution. It's *people!*

Building a great team allows you to leverage the time, skill, energy, and experience of others to take your business to millions of dollars. Remember, solve every problem and opportunity by thinking *"who and what systems,"* not *how.*

But as you likely know, it's not that easy. Your team can be your greatest source of leverage or your biggest frustration. For most six figure entrepreneurs, it's often the latter. I know it was for me.

In this chapter we are going to break down some systems and strategies to help make your team a major strength and set you up for years to come. This is an essential step that, if you get right, will be life-changing. So let's get you set up for big success with a truly world-class team.

The Secret Team Hack

While we don't want your business to center around you, you still play a critical role for your team. In fact, it all starts with you and this is the first major key to a world-class team.

You have to make the shift to take on responsibility. *You* are responsible for their success. *You* are responsible to make sure they have the systems, training, support, feedback, and infrastructure to thrive.

It is *your* responsibility to make things so clear and easy that they cannot fail!

Most entrepreneurs are so busy *doing, doing, doing* that they don't make much of any time for their team. But getting the right people set up for success is one of the single best forms of leverage you can have. IF you do it right.

To get to seven figures, you have to make this shift. Stop hoping for unicorns and make it your responsibility to help them succeed.

Think of McDonald's. They have the training, systems, and processes in place to make it easy for any average Joe off the street to make a Big Mac just as well as anyone else! And they can do so with speed and accuracy.

McDonald's has mastered making things turnkey, and it's one of many reasons why they are one of the top companies in the world.

Now, you don't have to be McDonald's to use this mentality and take *responsibility* for your team's success. Put the training, systems, and infrastructure in place so you can hire *good* people and **make them great!**

Want to have your team perform at a much higher level?

Make things so simple…so clear…so easy that your team cannot fail.

It's your responsibility.

I know what you're thinking, *"But Austin, I don't have the time to do any of those things."*

That's why the book is in this order—to show you how to free up time first, because you *do,* in fact, have time! You're just not using it properly.

But imagine how well your team could do if they were properly trained. Imagine if you helped them with the systems they need to do their job at a high level. What would that mean for your company long-term?

It's a priceless shift to make…and one that will keep you free from the weeds.

It's easy to blame your team. It's easy to be frustrated with them, knowing they're not doing things as well or as fast as you can. But you can choose to feel special or choose to be successful.

The successful CEO is one that sets their team up to WIN!

So, take responsibility. Make the time. Follow the steps in this book to take your systems, training, onboarding, feedback, and communication to the next level…and make your team great.

Your business growth will soon follow.

6-Figure Hustler	7-Figure CEO
• Always blaming your team for things not getting done as well as you could do them • Expects others to know what you know • Too busy to support team, thus indirectly setting them up to fail	• Takes responsibility for team success • Builds a team for the long-term, training and developing them over time • Understands the importance and cost of getting hiring right • Leads with systems and strong guidance with the intention to have them to be able to thrive without you

Your Most Important Sales And Marketing

The right people on your team can change *everything* for your business.

Which means that by far...

The most important sales and marketing you can do is with your hiring.

When we hire, it's exactly the same as if we were doing a big marketing promotion. We use a sales page for the job ad, run paid ads to it, send numerous emails, and follow up with candidates like they're our most important leads.

Because they are!

A great team will change your life and business, so take it seriously.

The vast majority of six-figure entrepreneurs, however, are *too busy* to make time for this. They rush hiring, put up a generic job description, and pray that a unicorn finds it. Then they're surprised when they end up with a mediocre team.

You want A-players, so do what will get an A-player's attention! For your next hiring push, here's what to do to get a lot more high-quality candidates:

1 - The Vision

Everything starts with the vision and mission of the company. High-performers aren't looking for a *job*. In this day and age, people are searching for meaning now more than ever. They yearn for that connection and mission—especially top-performing people who have lots of options for what they could do.

They are looking to be a part of something. So give them that opportunity!

Share the vision and mission of the company, and create something much bigger than just a boring old job. Where are you headed? Why does it matter?

Whether you're selling coaching programs or accounting services or anything else, it doesn't matter—**create a compelling future** that will get the right people you want to hire fired up to join you.

2 - The Campaign

Then, once you're clear on the exact role you're hiring for, build out a launch strategy with how you're going to market this position. What's your plan of attack? How are you going to get more of the *right* candidates than ever before?

It starts with a simple strategic plan. Just putting a job posting up is not a strategy! Be intentional about this.

3 - The Setup

For years, we've used a long-form sales page and converted it into a hiring page. I highly recommend that you do this, as well. You can use our template (7-Figure Toolkit: 2X.co/toolkit). The key is to sell the role in detail to your perfect hire. Include more about the role, responsibilities and results, skills needed, and of course more about the team and mission of the company.

Not only are you qualifying them to find the best candidate, you are constantly selling this role. It's your most important sales and marketing so treat it that way with your hiring assets.

4 - Positioning

A-players don't just work for *anybody*. They want to work for a place that matters. For a place that has something going for it. For a company that is winning.

So, positioning yourself in the right way is key. Here's why this matters so much:

a) People want to be proud of where they work. They want to share it with their family and friends, and having the right public positioning (and reputation) goes a *long* way in this subtle but required step.

b) You have a split second to make an impression on your candidates in the hiring process, and not many things will turn them off quite like bad positioning.

c) You'll get a lot fewer referrals of good candidates if the positioning isn't there. Everyone wants to protect their name/word and won't send someone to a company that looks unimpressive.

We'll talk about Million Dollar Positioning™ in detail in Chapter 7, but not only does the right positioning have an impact on your sales and marketing, even more importantly, it means a lot in your recruiting.

5 - Social Proof

Not many things sell quite like social proof. Just like you would for selling a program, get some quotes and endorsements from your current team and clients to show the candidates that you're the real deal.

"2X is an amazing company - from the mission of helping double the number of businesses that get to a 7 and 8 figure company - to the world class team - to the client results and success stories. Our clients are changing the world."

Tom Sylvester
2X, Director of Fulfillment

Nobody does this in hiring, but that makes it easy to differentiate yourself from their other options!

6 - Market Hard

Then, when these pieces are all in place, it's time to go live. Do a big push, making it exciting and fun, and add some urgency. You'll see more (and better) candidates than ever coming in.

Does this all sound like more work? Yes, it *is* more work…initially. But doing hiring right will save you years of time down the road and have you achieving exponentially more. Even just a couple A-players will change your business forever, so take it seriously and use these tips to stand out in the marketplace.

It's the most important marketing and sales you can do, hands down.

6-Figure Hustler	7-Figure CEO
• Doesn't put much effort or strategy into recruiting or hiring; is often too busy to spend time on this (even though it's of utmost importance) • Puts a job posting up and "hopes" to find a unicorn • Doesn't have a compelling vision that would stop an A-Player in their tracks to be interested in the role or company • As a result, doesn't have a lot of qualified candidates to choose from	• Understands cost and value of hiring right…and treats recruiting and hiring as the most important sales and marketing you can do • Positions company not only for sales and marketing, but also for hiring • Recruits attentively and intentionally to fill role; doesn't just sit back and wait • Sells the vision each step of the way in recruiting and hiring

No More Babysitting

Does anybody like micro-managing others?

I sure don't. It's pretty much adult babysitting. Your team doesn't want that, and you sure don't either. Instead, what you need is **leadership and management by design**.

You need to set up the infrastructure to create autonomy, great communication, and *speed* of execution.

The top problem in teams often centers on communication. The second problem is clarity. And the third is accountability.

Or better yet, the top problems are related to a lack of all three.

So how do we fix these issues?

First, it starts with *you*. (Noticing a trend here yet?)

You have to improve your communication. You need to make things clearer for everyone. You have to make commitments and hold yourself accountable. And you have to lead the way in turning your business into a machine with these principles I'm sharing with you.

That is all mission critical. It starts with you.

To help you lead by design, here are a few critical elements to help your team dramatically. Let's break them down.

1 - KPIs

To recap, key performance indicators are the critical metrics of progress toward an intended result. They're essential—not just for your business, but also for your team.

They tell you the facts of your business and the health of each step of your Value Chain and department.

Once you identify which metrics matter most, track them regularly, assign an owner to each one so that you can offload the responsibility of driving and improving that metric, and then hold your team accountable to them just like you would yourself. Now your team is clear and aligned on what the output is. It's wild how few entrepreneurs get their team clear on the metrics.

Everyone should have a few metrics that they're tied to—either metrics directly related to work they own (we call these primary metrics), or secondary metrics their work impacts that they should still be familiar with.

But having a number by itself doesn't mean much. What you want to see is improvement and consistency for each key metric. So, you need to track data over time to see the full picture.

Plus, you need to set a target goal that you're aiming for. Keep the targets conservative, as you want to set your team up for success. Again, it's about consistency and improvement. Not overnight success.

So start by tracking these regularly to monitor trends and issues. Most metrics will be great to track and update weekly. Have the owner of each metric (not you!) provide updates on the results and their plan of attack to improve as needed. This is a game-changing shift, as you're then empowering and leading by the numbers.

2 - The Daily Huddle

This is one meeting that changes everything—and it takes 15 minutes or less.

Done right, this meeting improves communication, focus, accountability, team planning, and efficiency. Long story short, this is a must.

This is a quick 8- to 15-minute meeting to run through:

1. Quick numbers update—check in on the top KPIs to refocus everyone on the objective
2. Everyone's top focus for the day—the most important priorities they're going to complete
3. "Stucks"—quick questions, needs, or things they're behind on to discuss
4. End with clarity—wrap up quickly with clear next steps, reminder of the current big focus, and momentum so everyone is focused and set for a great 24 hours until your next huddle

This meeting is fast, focused, and has you able to effectively manage (and hold accountable) your team.

Train everyone to bring their questions and challenges to this meeting to discuss and solve at once. This reduces reactivity and gets everyone aligned all at once. Then everyone is off to the races to execute. You included!

So block it off and get a daily huddle started immediately if you don't already do it. For small teams under seven people, we recommend one daily huddle. But as your team grows it'll likely break into department huddles.

Regardless, this is the most important meeting. Make it a part of your culture, and your team performance will improve immediately.

3 - The Job Scorecard

I originally learned about the concept of a Job Scorecard in *Who* by Randy Street and Geoff Smart.

We adapted this thinking to design a system that is specific for six- and seven-figure businesses. And now it is at the heart of every position we have on our team.

It's worth going into detail on this, so let's break down the full Job Scorecard in detail in the next section.

6-Figure Hustler	7-Figure CEO
• Spends a lot of time babysitting, micro-managing, and fixing team issues • Doesn't have true accountability • Team isn't super clear on their role, responsibilities, or key metrics they can lead • Inconsistent communication and leadership	• Understands the big common team problems of communication, clarity and accountability, and sets the structure to make those strengths (not weaknesses) • Creates other leaders, develops them over time, playing the long game • Leads by the numbers, and also helps use them to hold the team accountable • Creates a culture of great communication and rhythm; not reactivity • Leverages daily huddles to keep everyone aligned, focused, and humming • Gives objective feedback regularly to consistently help them improve

The Job Scorecard

Do you ever get frustrated that your team just isn't performing? You know they can do it. And you know they *want* to succeed.

But the reasons they aren't performing up to their potential come back to you as the leader. It is your responsibility to set them up for success. In nearly every small business we've worked with, we see these team issues:

- They aren't clear on exactly what is expected of them (even if it's clear to you).
- They aren't empowered and given full ownership over their work (fearing that you are going to fix it anyway).
- They're pulled in too many directions (most of which aren't their highest-impact responsibilities).
- And they aren't held accountable.

The Job Scorecard changes all of that. It's the centerpiece for every role, and needs to be for your team, as well.

We use it before and during the hiring process, and every month thereafter for as long as they're a part of our team. It's the roadmap for their role and helps drive clarity and better communication so that each employee can thrive.

There are five major elements in the Job Scorecard. You can also download our exact spreadsheet template we use in your 7-Figure Toolkit at: 2X.co/toolkit.

1 - Role Vision

The Job Scorecard begins in the same way we began this book: with a vision.

> *What's the high-level vision for this role? How does it fit into the overall picture? What is the big picture success?*

With this general direction for the role, we can define the specifics. But always start with the vision and define success.

Vision for the Role	To help XYZ Media Inc. get to consistent $300k+ / month by {date} by leading operations and project management, helping free Jesse up from internal management duties, optimizing internal systems and team performance to have a scalable, well-oiled machine that can continue the growth for years to come.

2 - *Their* Vision

This is a crucial step that most entrepreneurs skip. But if you want top talent, and you want to keep them for a long time, this is essential.

You have to get clear on what *they* want, too.

What are *their* goals? What do they want to achieve within their role? In what areas do they want to develop?

And how does their vision match up with the company's vision and where you're headed? We call this the Vision Crossover.

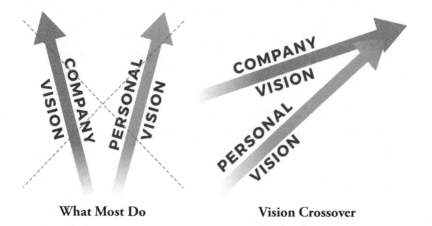

What Most Do   **Vision Crossover**

This is essential for long-lasting, win-win employee relationships.

WORLD-CLASS TEAM | 167

Have them define what success is for them and keep it front and center so that you can support them to make it happen. Because…

The more successful they are, the more successful you and the company are.

If their vision isn't aligned with the company's at all, then it's not a good fit. So understanding this early and ongoing is key.

Again, to make the next step as a leader, you have to make the mindset shift that your responsibility is to set them up for success. So get clear on their goals and growth, and set them up to win to get there in a way that's aligned with the company's mission and vision.

Do this, and you'll have a world-class team that goes above and beyond, and everyone wins.

Have your employees fill this in and review it with them monthly. This leads to a great conversation and makes their job much more than just a job; it's a mission. The shift is huge.

Personal Success *My role will be an absolute success if...*
    1. XYZ Media is operating with 0% reactivity
    2. Team members are happy and clear within their roles and responsbilities
    3. XYZ is completing sprint Rocks to 100%
    4. XYZ is viewed as a world-class company internationally
    5. Jesse removed from daily operations saving 15+ hours per week

Development *Key topics to learn and areas I want to develop in...*
    1. Operations required to scale a business past $5 million and then up to $10 million
    2. Efficient and simple project management (honing my current skills)
    3. Team development: how to create paths for people to level up

3 - Role Responsibilities

Next, define the top three to seven responsibilities of this person in their role. What will they lead and own in this role?

For instance, an operations manager might have the following top role responsibilities:

1. Internal Operations and Systems Lead
2. Project Management Lead
3. Hiring Lead
4. Numbers and Data Tracking
5. Head of HR

For each responsibility, include a few sub-bullets to further define the role and what's expected. Here's an example:

Responsibility
1. XYZ Operations Optimization & Systems Lead
- Oversee Asana and ensure all departments are utilizing for PM
- Lead all major internal meetings
- Ensure Rocks are planned and on pace
- Keep Playbook up to date
- Oversee creation, use of, and optimization of systems/processes
- Lead project management on all major initatives
- Ensure each department has a short and long term plan of action

2. Overall Team Optimization & Performance
- Ensure everyones scorecards are up to date
- Create improvement plan for all team members based on reviews

These specifics clarify what needs to be covered in monthly reviews and provide a clear picture of how well someone is doing and where they can improve.

4 - KPIs

How are employees expected to win the game if they don't know how the score is being measured? They won't.

Track the top handful of metrics for their role, and review these results with them during your monthly one-on-one check-ins.

The numbers take out the stories and tell the facts of what's working, what's not, where to focus and what to fix. From here, you can see objectively how they're performing and make a game plan for how to improve.

This feels like work at the beginning, but it's game-changing and ultimately helps employees drive big results in their roles. So, define the top metrics for each role, make sure they understand them and their responsibility with each, then track and review these in detail, and your results will rise to the next level if you have the right people in place.

5 - Monthly Review

It's been hinted at throughout the chapter, but the final section of the Job Scorecard is where you do a full-on monthly performance review. This feedback opens the lines of communication and gets you and your employees on the same page so you can help them optimize their roles.

The general order of the review is:

1. A self-assessment completed by the employee before the meeting on the Job Scorecard
2. The manager's review and comments, including rating and defining improvements and next month's success
3. A one-on-one meeting with their manager to discuss their full Job Scorecard in detail and get them clear on the month ahead

With this structure, you can have a good, objective and detailed conversation to help them improve each and every month. These are some of the most valuable meetings of your entire month, so make them a habit.

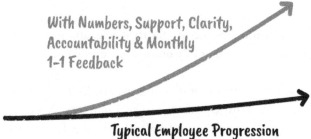

With Numbers, Support, Clarity, Accountability & Monthly 1-1 Feedback

Typical Employee Progression

Use our Job Scorecard template as your guide because the right setup makes this so much easier. Get instant access to it in your 7-Figure Toolkit (2X.co/toolkit). Inside that you'll see the tab for how to complete the monthly review, including core values and other feedback elements.

Remember, your team *wants* to do great. They want to perform. Set them up for success by using this Job Scorecard to give them much-needed clarity, support, accountability, and feedback.

Then watch them perform like never before!

6-Figure Hustler	7-Figure CEO
• Doesn't use job scorecards or give the team great clarity... on their role, what's expected of them, or how they'll be measured • Doesn't have accountability • No set cadence to review team performance and help them improve • Not clear on employee's vision and goals, and doesn't paint the long-term employee roadmap	• Has clear, written job scorecard with each role defined • Team is clear on their role, responsibilities, and how they'll be measured • Grades and measures employee performance regularly, improving and progressing each month • Alignment of vision between employee and company; great fit for each other

Crafting A Culture

Something that just isn't talked about nearly enough in small business that has a surprisingly massive impact is your *culture*.

The vast majority of six-figure companies are merely trying to survive; their focus is elsewhere, not on creating something like 'culture.'

It's a shame because not much else has a bigger and better impact long-term. Because with the right culture:

- You attract the right people and repel the wrong ones
- You embed the key principles so that your team executes based on certain principles
- You get people to focus on certain areas and drive more results
- And you create something much bigger than just yourself (or any single employee), creating an organism that can run itself— which is your goal long-term anyway!

To craft your culture, start with two core things: the vision and values of the company.

We've talked about the vision in Chapter 1. Now, define what your Core Values are of your company. These describe who you are as a company. They are its DNA—what it stands for.

Then, once you have these, use them every day to craft the culture you need.

You should be able to hire, fire, and lead based on the core values alone.

So, think about your DNA and what key principles that your company should live by. Brainstorm these by yourself, as well as with your team. Then simplify it down to the top 5 to 10 words or phrases that represent who you are going to be.

Here's an example of our 2X core values:

Then, for each value, create a short paragraph that describes it in detail, like this:

> ### *THE TEAM, THE TEAM, THE TEAM*
> It's hard to do big things by yourself—so don't. At 2X, we know the way you build a movement is with people, a vision, and a common goal. We pride ourselves on running like a well-oiled machine, working together as *one* to make the impossible a reality. We always put the team first, communicating and supporting each other like family. We work daily as a tribe moving toward the same mission, and we know that done right, 1+1+1 equals 10. Together we are unstoppable.

Once you have core values like these defined for your company, do what few businesses do—use them!

Praise people when they represent the values. We do this publicly in meetings as well as in a dedicated Slack channel for core values shoutouts.

Add them to everyone's Job Scorecards and review how they're performing for each one. Then discuss these with them each month, as these are what you want to live out each day.

And also talk about these in your meetings. We start and end every full team meeting with the values. They are our guide, and they're everywhere for the team to know.

First Slide Of Our Monthly Team Meeting

Remember, you should be able to hire, fire, and lead purely by the core values alone. Make them central to how you work day in and day out, and it will create a culture that ultimately fuels itself, transforming your company into a real, sustainable, high-performing business.

6-Figure Hustler	7-Figure CEO
• The culture isn't defined • No core values defined; if they are, they're generic and not fully unique to your DNA or not used regularly • No clear, compelling vision or purpose behind the company • "Too busy" to make time for things that have a long-term impact	• Strategically designing a culture to create the team and environment needed to achieve the vision • Core values and culture clearly defined and understood • Regularly share and use core values to truly create the culture • Can hire, fire, and lead by these core values alone

The All-Important Test Drive

Do you think you're a good judge of talent?

Sure you do! We all think that we're pretty good at understanding who will be good and who will not.

Yet, studies show that only 20% of hires actually turn into A-performers!

A big reason why is that people are at their best in the interview process. They tell you what you want to hear, highlighting the best snippets of what they have done and can do.

But you can't just let them *tell* you how great they are... You need them to *show* you.

In our hiring process, we do that in several ways.

1 - Test Tasks

The first key step is to not only ask them questions in the interview process, have them do things. Give them specific test tasks that allow you to see how their mind works, how they communicate, their attention to detail, and more. This is eye-opening every single time.

You can see an example and swipes of our test tasks in the 7-Figure Toolkit (2X.co/toolkit). We usually do 3 to 5 simple tasks that test multiple skills related to that position. We do this before our final interviews, and you'll quickly see the top candidates separate themselves from the pack.

Do this and trust me, you'll make exponentially better hiring decisions and save yourself countless hours and resources.

2 - Reference Checks

Mishiring is one of the costliest things in business—in money, time, frustration, distraction, opportunity cost. One study from the classic hiring book by Brad Smart, *Topgrading,* showed that the cost of a mis-hire is 5–27 times their salary. That's right, 5–27 times!

So a very simple key to get one more data point is with reference checks. The vast majority of small businesses don't do these. But they'll save you a lot of heartache and can be done fairly quickly.

I recommend that you talk to 2-3 people and ask them the hard questions. Get the real insight on their strengths, weaknesses, why they left (to match stories), if they'd hire them, what role they're perfect for, if they think the candidate is a fit for the role you're hiring for, and more. A ~15 minute chat can go a long way and give you caution or confidence.

Make it an essential part of your hiring process!

3 - The Trial Period

Once we narrow it down to the top person that we want to bring on, it isn't done just yet. There's one more step: a short-term trial period.

For some roles this is two weeks. For others it could be longer or shorter, but the key is to have a clear and objective way to make sure it's a great fit for both sides.

This is a systematic way to 'hire slow, fire fast'—which is a business maxim you've heard many times for a reason!

At this point, the new hire is brought onto the team in a paid role. This trial is when things get *real* because they're done talking a good game and are now expected to drive some results—even if just in a very small way. We start with general onboarding and training to get them up to speed, but as quickly as possible we get them on a few tasks or projects to start to see how they'd fit in long-term.

Some will crumble, some will thrive, and it never takes long to see if you have an A-player on your hands! A few things to look for in this period are:

Core Values Fit

Will they fit the team and culture? How will they mesh with the team? If they're not a core values fit, it's an easy "no," no matter how much you need to fill a role.

Results

You aren't looking for them to change your company and drive a ton of growth in the blink of an eye, but you are looking for their output.

> Do they complete the exact things you laid out for them? Do they help improve some results in their department? Do they provide tangible value?

Outline and share the exact expectations during their trial period, including how you're going to decide on them at the end of the trial. Don't have them guess. Lay it out in specific detail. Once they know the game and the stakes, see what they accomplish. It is always clear if they perform (as long as you define success like I mentioned).

Responsibility Capabilities

Before hiring, fill out a complete Job Scorecard with:

- Role responsibilities: what they'll be responsible for in the day-to-day
- KPIs they'll be responsible for owning or supporting the results for

Then evaluate them on both of those at the end of the trial. Do they show the ability to handle this role and drive the results necessary?

As entrepreneur Derek Sivers said,

"If you're not saying "HELL YEAH!" about something, say no."

That is definitely the case in hiring!

Red Flags

Are there any red flags that your new hire might not work? This is important to identify *now*.

Rarely do red flags just go away. So be skeptical. Look out for signs of mismatch and make the right decisions for the long term. And address these head-on.

Most are afraid to have difficult conversations, so they sweep things under the rug. But a trial run is the time to address any concerns and make the tough decisions early. Skip past this and you'll soon regret it.

If you aren't very much sold on a candidate, then by all means, do not hire that person. Your hiring mentality needs to be, *"No matter how long it takes, I will find the right person!"*

This will be tough in the moment as you try to fill a role and see the potential in someone. But if they don't test well and pass the above tests, keep looking. It is far more expensive to hire the wrong person.

I love the question, ***"Knowing what you know now, would you enthusiastically hire that person if you did it all over again?"*** If the answer to this after a short trial isn't 100% *YES*, then it's a no. Keep looking.

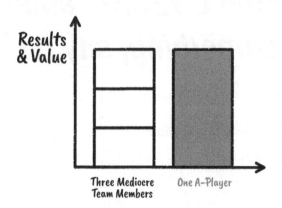

Remember, one A-player is worth three mediocre ones, so 'hire slow, fire fast' and use these two test periods to make sure you bring on the right people one at a time.

If you do, you'll have a world-class team and be on the fast-track to millions.

6-Figure Hustler	7-Figure CEO
• Don't test candidates in the interviewing process • Hire quickly and not very thoroughly • No consistent hiring process in place • Use gut and intuition as primary tools for hiring, not objective measurement	• Objectively test candidates in hiring process, having them jump through multiple hoops to prove their worth • Have strategic onboarding to get new employees up to speed fast • Use a trial period to ensure right candidates are hired, leveraging a system for "hire slow, fire fast" • Understand the importance of waiting and working for the right candidate, not hiring just to fill a role in a rush

Solutions, Not Monkeys

You want solutions, not monkeys.

Monkeys are problems. They're other people's challenges and the extra things you take on.

If you're anything like where I've been in the past, everyone on your team brings these monkeys to you.

It gets exhausting!

Then, eventually you'll realize:

You are actually the one that creates the culture of everyone bringing their problems to you! And secondly…

You can't get to where you really want to go in business if you are the only leader.

If everyone is just doing what you tell them and totally reliant on you, then that's not a business, that's a self-employed job that is dependent on your time and talent.

If you stop, they pretty much stop. This is what most six-figure entrepreneurs unknowingly do.

They create their team to be followers, and train others that they'll answer all of the questions for them! Then they're shocked when people don't magically start running and driving results *without* them.

But to get where you want to go, to create a business that drives growth, big income, lots of opportunities, and a ton of **freedom**, you need a team of people that can make decisions and drive results within their roles.

The good news is, you can start to train your team to be leaders with just a few simple words. Anytime someone brings you a problem or question, simply ask them:

"What would you suggest we do?"

These six words will have you going from having a bunch of followers and more *monkeys* you have to deal with to having people who start to think for themselves. They start to problem-solve, and they soon realize they know more than they thought!

They then won't need you as much, which is good news for you (freedom!), for them (autonomy!), and for the business (growth!). This is a huge win-win, and starts with a simple question.

Soon, they build confidence to solve problems themselves. By doing so, they save you time and energy, they keep things off of your plate, and all of this adds up to exponentially more performance by all.

You pay your team to drive results and solutions. Now train them to do just that strategically!

Solutions, not monkeys. It's a game-changing leadership hack.

6-Figure Hustler	7-Figure CEO
• Takes on everyone else's problems (often unknowingly) • Teaches team to come to you for their problems and solutions • Too busy to train and develop your team, so you stay in this cycle of them requiring you	• Works to create other leaders • Leverages the simple question, *"What would you suggest we do?"* • Teaches others to become problem solvers and teaches them the *why* behind things so they can ultimately make strong decisions without you

The Two Roles To Keep You FREE

With over 80% of the six-figure businesses we've worked with, the first two roles we focus on to maximize are the same. Take note, because these are likely the first two roles you should make sure you nail, as well.

#1: The Number One for Numero Uno

In my early career working for a big oil company, I had a short stint in sales. There, I worked with and got exposed to a lot of small businesses. That's where I learned a very important lesson:

Every great small business has a great assistant.

It's a must.

This was the first hire I made starting out years ago. I went from assistant to assistant with one horrible experience after another—until I struck gold. After that, **everything changed for me and my business.**

I once asked marketing expert Billy Gene what the pivot point was for how he went from zero to nearly $1 million *per month* in just four years. His answer: It started with getting an assistant!

His mentor, Cameron Herold, told him, *"If you don't have an assistant, you are the assistant."*

It's so true. The opportunity cost of your time is so high as you scale to seven figures and beyond, so start by offloading the admin stuff.

I have gotten so much out of having an assistant that I now have two virtual assistants as well as a part-time in-person house assistant, too. They are three of the most important people for my life and business.

This is often the highest-impact role you can hire for. Start here, and get ready for your life to change.

#2: Operations Manager

The big goal is to get you out of the day-to-day operations and focused on your zone of genius.

Often the key hire after an assistant is someone to manage operations and fulfillment. Depending on your business, this could be:

- Operations Manager
- Account Manager
- Client Manager
- Project Manager
- Fulfillment Manager

Someone needs to help oversee and execute tasks so that you can stay focused on growth.

Handling the day-to-day operations that need to happen, or managing clients or fulfillment can take so much energy and time, and doesn't have to be done by you. In fact, most of the time it *shouldn't* be done by you. So identify your biggest need related to operations and/or fulfillment, and fill that role with the right person.

These two roles are the 80/20 of getting you out—and keeping you out—of the weeds. Get these right, and you'll have a much easier time scaling to seven figures fast.

6-Figure Hustler	7-Figure CEO
• Still stuck in most of the administrative and operations tasks • Doesn't have a great assistant to help support • Isn't great at delegating or developing, which makes it tough to find a rockstar to help you	• Know the impact of having the right admin and operations support so you can grow • Have a world-class assistant keeping you free from the weeds • Have operations/project/fulfillment support to keep you free from the day-to-day operations

Chapter 5 Big Ideas

- Take the responsibility to set your team up for success, giving them the time, support, and guidance so they can succeed. Don't expect them to be superheroes; take the responsibility to help *make* them great. Systems will help!

- Go all-out in recruiting and hiring, knowing that one high performer is worth three or more mediocre ones! Treat your recruiting and hiring as your most important sales and marketing... because it is.

- Leverage a job scorecard to get your employees clear and aligned, hold them accountable, and give objective feedback regularly to help them improve.

- Ensure you understand your team's personal vision and goals too, finding the right people who can be a part of your team for the long-term. Use this to have the *vision crossover*.

- Strategically craft your culture and core values to help you create the team and execution needed to make your vision a reality.

- Hire, fire, and consistently lead by the core values to fully make this culture a reality.

- Create a system to 'hire slow, fire fast' using test tasks and a trial period for new hires.

- Have the mentality, *'No matter how long it takes, I will find the right person!'*

- You can't get to where you want to go if you're the only leader.

- Don't just answer questions; train your team to bring solutions by leveraging the simple question, *"What would you suggest we do?"*

- The key role to hire for is a world-class personal or virtual assistant.

CHAPTER 6

CLOSE!

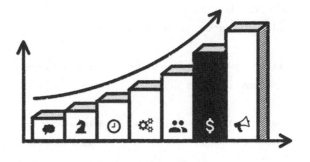

The Quickest Levers To Scale

When we start working with a business, there are a few quick wins we go after that help them scale to the next level. A few of these are:

- Freeing up time (as with the proper time you can achieve anything)
- Maximizing LTV (through products/offers, price, retention, and the right models)
- Tapping into the "goldmine" (more on that soon)

And of course…

Nailing your sales conversions.

Improving sales conversions to convert new and existing leads at a higher, faster rate is one single lever that has a massive ripple effect across your cash flow, marketing, and entire business.

And the cool thing is, it's often quite easy to make a big impact. That's what this chapter is all about.

If we do nothing else but help you increase your sales conversions from, for example, 10% to 15%—keeping the same number of leads, the same price, the same LTV, and everything—then you grow your business by 50%!

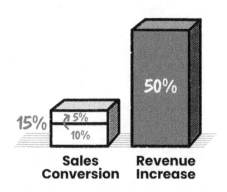

One lever. Massive impact.

And with the right systems and strategies, you should make sales a major strength. Here's how to make it happen.

Know Your Damn Numbers

After reading this book, there are a few major takeaways I want to make sure you never forget. This is one of them:

Know your damn numbers.

As Robert Kiyosaki says, *"The faster you want to get rich, the more accurate with numbers you must be."*

This is especially true in sales.

When we encounter any business challenge, we follow a process guided by three key questions:

1. What's the goal (the end result we're after)? (Vision & Targets)

2. What is the current reality (the actual KPIs)? (Numbers)

3. Based on the numbers, what are the exact issues and opportunities to improve? What are the key levers and plan of attack? (Strategy)

Vision, numbers, strategy. The numbers are your key to help you get to that big vision of yours. They take out the guesswork and make it clear what's going well and what is not. From there, the solutions become easy.

This is no different for your sales department. In fact, this is even *more* crucial in your sales department. Before we get into the sales script or make any major tweaks to your pitch, this is where we go—to the numbers.

To help, what we do is break down your sales into smaller steps to see where the real bottleneck is. We call this a *micro* Value Chain.

For sales, your steps could look like this:

1. Application: Prospect applies to work with you on your website.
2. Schedule Call: If qualified, they schedule a sales meeting or call.
3. Show Up: They show up for the initial call.
4. Close: They buy your product/service.

You could look at just your sales conversions and see you have a big problem. But then, where would you begin? You'd be guessing, and likely working to fix the *wrong* thing.

On the other hand, if you have the steps broken out in detail, you can see exactly where the bottleneck is and can tackle it head-on. Remember, **the more clearly that you can identify the problem, the easier the solution becomes**. And the numbers are your guide to see that.

So break your full sales process into micro-steps and track the metrics that we discussed before: the actual, recent average, target goal, and ideally a minimum baseline goal.

	Application	Schedule Call	Show Up	Close
Actual	27	62%	78%	34%
Target	25	75%	80%	30%
Baseline	22	65%	72%	25%
Average (3 Mo.)	28	63%	76%	33%

With this clarity, you'll quickly see where the weak links are and have much better accountability for your team.

We see over and over how it can unlock growth. One example is 2X client Ryan Rockwell. He came into the 2X Accelerator with a lot of potential, but he was stuck at ~$374k per year in revenue. A big reason why is he didn't know his numbers at all. So, he was working hard trying to solve the wrong things, kept hiring and firing sales reps, and ultimately had to do most things himself. He said, *"When I came in, I didn't even know what KPI meant."*

While in the program, by first going deep into his numbers and improving his sales department to be a machine, he grew from $31k per month to $65k per month…to then over $307k per month! He 10X'ed once he fully executed what I'm sharing with you, and so much of that was driven by the numbers and his sales machine.

He added, *"Now we have literally dialed in so much on every single part of our business that we know exactly how to scale every step of the way. The future has never been brighter for us."*

So, long story short, if you want to fix your business and optimize *every* department (especially sales)… break things into a Value Chain series of steps, and use your numbers as the guide.

The rest becomes much easier from there.

6-Figure Hustler	7-Figure CEO
• Doesn't know exactly what part of the sales process is your bottleneck • Too busy to track the metrics • Often focusing on wrong KPIs • Doesn't hold sales team accountable	• Breaks down their sales into a micro value chain series of steps • Uses the numbers as the guide for where to focus and what to fix • Helps hold each sales rep accountable for results with the key metrics

Have A Process

Everything you do in your business should be a system. Everything.

Especially something as important as sales.

With the right sales process, you'll have more confidence and consistency, better forecasts, improved conversions, and you'll protect yourself against just relying on a rockstar salesperson.

To summarize: it's important!

Our full sales system has 17 elements, but the 80/20 of what you need to dramatically improve your sales team and conversions comes down to the *process*—**before, during, and after the sales attempt.**

So, we'll break down what to focus on for each of these three now to maximize conversions and make sales a major strength in your company.

Pre-Sale: The '80% Sold' Rule

Imagine that your sales team *only* talks to hot, qualified, pre-sold leads that have seen your best content and top case studies, and they know what you offer.

> *What would that mean for your sales team?*
> *What about your conversion rates?*
> *What about your confidence in scaling your marketing?*

It would be game-changing, right?

It is. And it's possible. Just use our 2X '80% Sold' rule and get your sales team set up for success.

The goal with this is to have your leads be at least 80% pre-sold on your product/service before they ever get a pitch and price. This makes the sales experience so much easier and smoother, plus you don't have to rely on crazy sales tactics.

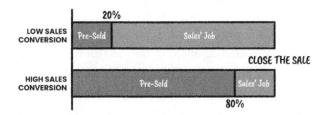

So let's strategically map out how you can get your prospects 80% sold. Here are a few key things to take into account:

1 - Inflict Pain

What you want to do in your marketing and lead-up to the sale is nail their problem and situation. You want them to be thinking, *"Yes, you made this for me. That is exactly my situation!"*

Touch on their key challenges, inflict some pain so they are even more interested to make a change, and show that you have the specific solution they need. If you know and understand them, you are in a prime position to help them change.

2 - Authority Positioning

Next, you need to be trusted. Why should they listen to you? Your prospects need to see you as the authority in your niche.

One thing we do is send leads to a couple videos that explain some of our key methodologies. This touches on some of their pain points and why they're stuck not growing their business. Even more importantly, we give a lot of value and show that we have the solution that will forever solve their pain.

Whether this is an article, FAQ, video, book, or anything else, it's a good idea to consider how you can further position yourself as the go-to credible authority *before* the sale.

3 - Explain The Offering

If you wait until the pitch to explain the offer, your leads have a lot to digest. Explain your offering ahead of time so that it's not a shock. They should know going into the pitch what it is you do and how you can help them. They don't need to know all of the specifics, but they should have a solid idea.

In the pitch you can then explain the key points that they need to know, but too much nuance and new information can cause confusion. And confused prospects don't buy!

So think: is it clear what you offer and how you help customers? And how can you keep the pitch simple and clear so there isn't the opportunity for too much new information? Make it clear, simple, and powerful and you'll be set up to win.

4 - Objection Squashing

It's simple:

Figure out the top objections… And squash them *before* they come up!

This is much easier and better than responding to objections after they're already firm in someone's mind.

I'll share more on objections later, but the key thing is to figure out your top objections and strategically address these in your marketing or pre-sales process. You can do this via client stories, in your authority positioning, as part of the *irresistible* offer, or more.

But think strategically of how you can plant the seed that those objections shouldn't be concerns and again, you'll make sales so much easier.

5 - Get Leads Hot

The last tip is to think strategically how you can get them excited and strike while the iron is hot.

They're an interested lead, so you should make it exciting to be there. If you delay too long after a prospect shows interest, you risk missing a sales opportunity. The common saying in sales is, *"Time kills all deals."*

Instead, show them social proof, get them excited, build that momentum—and strike while they're hot. Don't delay.

Now, think about your pre-sales process. Are you doing each of these five things? Strategically craft the ideal warm-up process, get leads '80% sold,' and make your sales team look like superstars. You'll notice the results immediately when you do.

6-Figure Hustler	7-Figure CEO
• No real strategic pre-sales warm up • Waits for objections to come up before handling them • Leaves a lot to be explained at sales presentation, making it complex to digest all at once, leading to indecision • Marketing and sales not working together to help set sales up for success	• Works with marketing to get prospects hot and ready, 80% or more pre-sold before getting to a sales presentation • Strategically builds value and anticipation for the prospect leading into a sale with momentum • Squashes objections before they come up with stories, examples, and value • Inflicts pain subtly to have prospect further desire what you sell (and urgency of it)

During Sale: Keeping Control

Sales is very much about *control*. As soon as you lose that, you likely lose the sale.

Because if the prospect has control, they'll ask a couple of general questions and immediately go straight to, *"What's the price?" and decide.*

(Unfortunately, it's usually a "no" at that point.)

So, you want to get control early and keep it. The longer it takes you to gain control, the harder it is to get it.

Three key elements can help you do this:

1 - The Script

You can't have control if you don't know where you're going.

Having a sales script—even a loose one—enables you to control the prospect through the sales process that *you* define.

This may feel restricting to some, but without the right flow, you might be sabotaging your sales conversions and missing out on *big* money! Trust me.

A good script and flow helps you and your sales reps strategically guide the prospect through an intentional conversation, keeping things on track and in control.

This could be a word-for-word script to follow or even some high-level bullets and questions to help you stay focused on what matters for the sales meeting. Just don't try to wing it, as most do.

The general sales process flow we suggest is:

A. **Meet & Greet** - Connect, break the ice, and start to build rapport.

B. **Qualification** - Make sure they're qualified before you spend time working them toward a sale. This is important to do early and plant the seed of what's to come. Plus, this is where your real discovery starts, asking them questions to inflict pain and understand how your solution is a great fit.

C. **Presentation** - This is the meat of your sales process, where you present how it is you can help solve their problem. The right presentation is crucial to make the benefits—not just the features of your service—clear. Once the benefits are specified, you can share the deliverables and the nuts and bolts.

D. **Trial Close** - Gauge where they're at, hot or cold, and if you can move on to the next phase. If they haven't seen enough value, then you have to go back to discovery and the benefits before you can proceed. A few simple questions can tell you if you're ready to move forward with the pitch. We will talk about these in more detail next.

E. **Price** - Deliver the price...and shut up. It's important to share the price with confidence and wait for them to respond. If you don't believe your product has enough value, there is no way your prospect will.

F. **Objection Handle** - You're probably getting the same common objections over and over, so let's have some techniques to handle these in stride, which we'll cover soon.

G. **Close** - Move them into a decision to buy.

This is a high-level overview, but you can get the full 2X Sales Script guide in your 7-Figure Toolkit (2X.co/toolkit).

2 - Trial Closes

The second way to maintain control is to lead the sales conversation from one stage to the next using something called a 'trial close.'

Trial closes are questions to gauge how your prospect is feeling that let you know where you are in the sales process, when you can proceed to the next step, and ultimately ask for the sale.

Before advancing to the next major part of the conversation, you have to gauge where they're at and see if they are ready to move there. If they aren't, you need to go back, ask more questions, and most importantly, build more value.

If your prospect isn't convinced on something, then you either haven't demonstrated the value of that benefit well enough, or you are emphasizing the wrong benefit.

A few examples of trial closes are:

Where do you see our product having the biggest impact?

How do you feel about what we've discussed so far?

Which option are you leaning toward so far; the {option 1} or the {option 2}?

You'll want to use these after your presentation or after a strong selling point. Their answers will tell you a lot, and you'll be able to see if you need to go back or proceed forward.

Trial close your way through your sales script, and you'll methodically guide them to a sale that you are both happy with. It's not high-pressure selling, just a win-win outcome with no buyer's remorse. That's what you're aiming for.

3 - Technique

Combine a great offer with a great sales system *and* good technique, and you instantly have some world-class conversions.

Here are a few strategies to have in your back pocket to make that happen:

- Use open-ended questions in the discovery and presentation to get them to talk, and then move to closed questions (where the answer is yes or no) when closing to move them toward a commitment.

- Probe for more information if you don't get enough. A few examples are: "What do you mean by that?", "Tell me more about…," and "When you say you tried {i.e., product}, what really stood out?"

- "The best close is a good open." Ask our head of sales, Pat Bennett, any questions about closing, and he will likely tell you this. The more time you spend opening, the less time you'll have to spend closing.

- Build urgency early. Having urgency really helps with getting people to decide one way or the other, so plant the seed early to get them pre-framed to make a decision.

- BAMFAM (book a meeting from a meeting): You should never leave a meeting without a clear next step. Don't leave it up to them to just 'get back to you.' Have a clear, tangible next step.

There are more sales techniques and training on exact scripts and verbiage to use in your 7-Figure Toolkit at 2X.co/toolkit.

Use these tools to keep control, and you'll reduce objections, increase closing rates, *and* make for a better sales experience for everyone involved.

6-Figure Hustler	7-Figure CEO
• Doesn't have a defined script or sales process • Different sales process used by different people; not duplicatable if you hired another person today • Doesn't qualify early, often wasting time with wrong leads • Reactive in the call, often letting the prospect guide the conversation with their questions	• Knows that control is key in the sales process • Uses a proven script optimized over time to strategically guide prospects in a good flow to a close • Qualify early on to minimize time with the wrong leads • Uses trial closes to ensure it's okay to move forward to next phase of sales conversation, improving both prospect experience and close rate

Post-Sale: Maximizing Conversions

The fortune is in the follow-up. You know this, or at least you've heard it before, but do you do it well?

From my experience, over 90% of our six- and seven-figure businesses are missing out on a *lot* of potential sales because they aren't effectively following up!

Numerous studies show that 80% of the sales happen after the fifth contact.[5] Yet those same studies show that the vast majority of sales reps give up after just a few contacts!

That means a huge portion of sales aren't happening due to bad or, more likely, nonexistent follow-up. It's no surprise that most struggle with sales!

Getting new leads is one of the most expensive things in business. So, the better that you do at nurturing and converting your leads will set you apart. And one surprisingly powerful lever is improving your follow up!

This one lever can effectively help you double your sales.

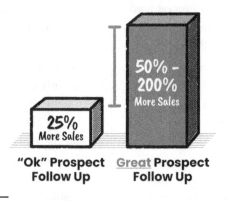

50% –
200%
More Sales

25%
More Sales

"Ok" Prospect
Follow Up

Great Prospect
Follow Up

5 Clay, Robert. "Why You Must Follow Up Leads." *Marketing Donut,* https://www.marketingdonut.co.uk/sales/sales-techniques-and-negotiations/why-you-must-follow-up-leads

Yes, you want to get them to decide early, but if they don't, they aren't lost. Continue to manage and nurture them, and at the right time, many will be ready.

The fortune is in the follow-up. But I'll take it one step further...

The Fortune - Part 2

The worst result is doing all this work, selling to a new ideal customer, only to have a poor experience right after they pay.

Unfortunately, this is all too common.

We celebrate the sale, and forget to do...

The most important sales of all: your current customers.

And that journey never ends. **Maximizing LTV by creating raving fans is an essential part of your multi-million dollar business**, and the post-sale immediate next steps is a huge key to start them off right. This protects against buyer's remorse and goes a long way in making a great first impression for their experience as a customer.

You want to have the exact steps smooth and clear so they are onboarded in a five-star way. This sets the tone for higher LTV, more referrals, greater success, easier clients, and more. Trust me, this goes a long way.

Get this right, and you'll be tapping into another huge source of revenue.

Remember, sales never ends. It's not a one-time thing. Think of the entire customer journey. The more that you and your sales team can continue to give value and make for a better experience before, during, *and* after the sales pitch the more that you'll see your business grow.

Play the long game and you'll be well on your way to many millions in the future.

<u>6-Figure Hustler</u>	<u>7-Figure CEO</u>
• Focuses only on short-term sales, and is more focused on the sale than the customer relationship • Doesn't have an effective follow-up system with prospects who say no • Upon purchase, doesn't have great systems to take care of new clients effectively	• Knows that the best lever to grow is LTV, ensuring the sales aren't done after the initial sale • Works to start clients fast and make them raving fan customers • Has good follow up systems in place to convert a good portion of prospects who don't purchase right away

Objection Kryptonite

The best way to handle objections is by addressing them *before* they come up. But even if this is a focus in your pre-sales process (using the '80% Sold' rule), objections will still come up, and you need to be ready to handle them.

The good news is, the same objections will come up over and over again, so you can be prepared to address them with confidence...and give prospects no reason but to say *yes* (and buy from you).

Depending on what you're selling, the most common objections that come up are likely related to:

- No time
- No money (or price)
- Not the right time (or not ready)
- Need to talk to partner, spouse, accountant, advisor
- Have to think about it
- Can do it themselves

There are some underlying reasons behind all of these reasons (there's not enough perceived value, they don't understand, or they don't fully trust you), but let's address them objectively for now.

I asked our head of sales, Pat Bennett, what he recommends you have in your arsenal to handle any objection like a pro. Here's what he shared:

1 - Anticipate

Based on a prospect's questions, body language, and answers, a good salesperson can anticipate what objections will come up.

Address them *before* they do, and you'll have much higher odds of having them believe you.

Objection Handle Success Rate

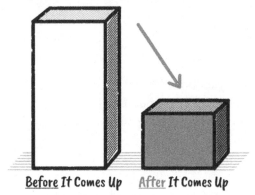

Before It Comes Up   **After** It Comes Up

If you wait until the lead verbalizes their objection, they gain *control*—and we learned how important control is earlier. Beating them to the punch goes a surprisingly long way. Anticipate their objections, stay calm, and get them back on the path to closing so they have no reason but to buy from you.

2 - Isolate

Most times, **the objection is really about the prospect not seeing enough VALUE** in what you're selling.

To address this, get to the root of the objection and isolate their *real* reason.

For instance, if the objection is price, you want to go deeper and see whether that's the real issue (meaning they don't have the money or budget for it), or whether they just don't see the true value.

If it really is a money issue, then you can counter with a payment plan or risk reversal (money-back guarantee). More often, it's related to value...

If the right prospect sees substantially more value than the price, they'll buy.

If they don't yet, you have to go back to discovery and uncover more pain and benefits to move them across the line.

3 - Feel. Felt. Found.

One of the best ways to handle objections is to get comfortable replying with the timeless technique, 'Feel, Felt, Found.' It goes like this:

I understand how you *feel*. (Acknowledge the objection.)

Most of my clients *felt* the same way. (Relate and connect, showing them others had the same concern.)

But you know what they *found*? (Explain the reality, re-emphasizing the benefits and outcomes they got and how this objection shouldn't be holding them back.)

You can use yourself as an example, but it's even better to use other customers to help them see how they're not alone and that they're objection is not a concern after all.

4 - If I could _____, would you _____?

After you isolate and get down to the root objection, then you can use this strategy to gauge whether that's the right issue keeping them from moving forward. Ask them, *"If I could [offer X incentive or option], would you leave a deposit today?"*

You must have an action and time commitment. You must have them make a decision (which way too many small business sales conversations don't do).

Another example is, if the objection is on price because they don't have $1,000 on hand to pay your down payment, you might learn they could do half of that and then ask, *"If I could get it approved for you to only pay a down payment today of $500 instead of $1,000, would you be ready to move forward today?"*

They'll either say yes, or they'll still be a no, and you'll have to go uncover the real objections holding them back and work back through the process.

Regardless, you know objections are going to come up. Anticipate them, stay calm and in control, isolate the root of the objection, use a few simple techniques to squash it in their mind, and get on to the close.

Done right, your prospects will have no reason but to say yes!

6-Figure Hustler	7-Figure CEO
• Doesn't track what the top objections are • Doesn't have a great response to handle objections • Gets thrown off of sales process when objections come up • Moves through the sales process without good awareness of where the prospect is at • Doesn't build enough value in the solution you offer	• Understands and is prepared for the top objections with a great handle • Has several techniques to uncover and reverse objections • Gets skilled at anticipating objections based on sales conversation, and addresses early • Handles objections in flow and naturally • Makes sure to build value each step of the way, maximizing the value to price ratio (and thus the odds of closing)

The Hidden Forces Of Great Sales Conversions

No matter what industry you're in, what product you're selling, and how you've been doing in sales, getting better and faster sales conversions comes down to the same elements.

Some are obvious like your sales script or objection handling skills. But the ones that matter even more are under the surface. Here are four somewhat hidden forces to have world-class conversions.

1 - Model ONE™

We stressed the importance of this early on because it changes so much (as in *everything*), from your business model to your team to your marketing and sales conversions.

- a. Start selling the right people…
- b. The right stuff…
- c. At the right price…
- d. With the right positioning…
- e. In a way that can scale.

Go deep into this as a top priority if you haven't already. It is the 80/20 of getting more traction than ever. And especially nail that #1: your ITA.

The more clear and targeted this is, the more narrow you can get with your offer, pain points, irresistible offer, objection management, and more. This is the 80/20 of the 80/20.

2 - Irresistible Offer

Related to your Model ONE™ strategy, but worth calling out is this secret weapon to make your sales team look like heroes: creating truly irresistible offers.

Follow the guide in Chapter 2 and you'll make your sales team's job exponentially easier, setting everyone up to win.

3 - Measurement

See: Know Your Damn Numbers.

Otherwise, you'll be guessing and likely working too hard on the wrong problems.

4 - Mindset

Most importantly of all, it all goes back to the right mindset.

Sales is a game of rejection, so you must have the proper mentality...

Or the best offer and greatest tools won't matter much!

Done right, everything in this chapter will help support your mindset, but here are a few additional key ways to make sure your sales rep's mindset is rock solid consistently:

- Protect your mindset at all costs. You won't have a 100% closing rate, but you must go into every presentation with the full expectation that you *will* close it. Just don't let the no's impact your mindset walking into your next presentation.

- Don't do it alone. Having a sales manager, or at the least, a great culture and team around you keeps you out of your head and in the right state of mind. Sales reps can get on an island separated from much of the team, so work to keep them involved. It'll benefit everyone. Plus, make it your sales manager's responsibility to protect the mindset of their sales team. This is a balance of driving results and accountability while supporting them and their mentality; not easy to do, but way better than driving a negative mindset, which helps nobody win.

- Give yourself a breather. Hitting the numbers and being active in sales is key, but going back-to-back without resetting can hurt your conversions in a big way. Plan some break time in between sales meetings to put your best foot forward and increase the odds of success, especially in high-ticket non-transactional sales.

- Get some wins on the board and build momentum. Sometimes, if you have multiple products, go and sell a few of the easier sales, even if they're not the most profitable, to get your mojo back.

And lastly…

By far the biggest thing with mindset is to get better at selling.

"Getting fewer no's is the best thing you can do," says Pat. When you are strong at sales, you get more sales, and that builds confidence and momentum.

The reverse of that is just as true, too! You don't get sales, that hurts your confidence, which gets you frustrated and desperate, then you bring that energy to your sales meetings, and your prospects can smell desperation from a mile away. So this leads to even fewer sales.

The compound effect either works for you or against you, so implementing everything from this chapter to have world-class sales conversions can get you on the fast-track to building more momentum and blowing past seven figures.

Take it seriously, implement each piece one by one, and turn your sales department into a closing machine.

6-Figure Hustler	7-Figure CEO
• Keeps fixing the surface level problems without going deeper	• Doesn't just fix the present problem, but most importantly goes back to the root causes
• Has a broad ITA, so are unable to fully dial in and duplicate the sales conversions	• Is really focused on nailing Model ONE™ with a clear, focused ITA to start
• Doesn't have irresistible offers	• Knows a major secret to great sales is an irresistible offer and how this makes everything else easier
• Doesn't objectively use the numbers as the guide of where to focus, what to fix, or to help optimize the team	• Uses the numbers as the guide
• Has an up-and-down mindset that impacts sales	• Is always working to protect and optimize the mindset of any sales team

Chapter 6 Big Ideas

- Sales conversions are one of the single best levers that have a positive ripple effect across your entire business.
- Know your damn numbers! Break down sales into a series of steps and track your key metrics to be able to pinpoint exactly where to focus and what to fix.
- Lead and manage by those metrics, holding your team accountable to the KPIs that matter most.
- Have a full sales system, including elements for before, during *and* after the sales pitch.
- Get prospects hot and pre-sold strategically using the "80% Sold" rule as you lead them into the closing opportunity.
- Squash the most common objections *before* they come up; and be ready for objections when they do with a few techniques.
- Have a script that you test and optimize over time to get the ideal flow, and keep control of the conversation, guiding prospects into the close.
- Maximize not only sales conversions but also customer experience and lifetime value by having effective follow up systems for those that do and do not buy! The sale is when the customer journey really begins.
- Don't just fix the surface level problems. Most importantly, go to the source with a dialed-in Model ONE™ strategy, irresistible offers, addressing the right bottleneck, and properly managing the mindset of your sales team.
- The best thing for your mindset is to get better at selling.

CHAPTER 7

GROWTH ENGINES

Marketing Is The Last Piece; Here's Why

At 2X, we've had some big results. At the time of this writing, our clients have generated over $255 million while still *in* our coaching programs during our first few years of business!

At the center of this success is what I learned from working with hundreds of entrepreneurs:

There is a very important and strategic *order* to things.

And in that order for small businesses, marketing is *not* what is most important…at least not to start!

When it comes to building a consistent, repeatable, fast-growing business that scales without your hours and grit, marketing is the last primary focus.

I know this may be a shock and it's counterintuitive to everything you've learned to date, but we've proven it over and over and over again.

Do you need marketing? Absolutely. No question about it. Without leads you wouldn't have a business. But to scale from six to seven figures, and do so FAST, the best thing you can do is have your primary focus be in the exact order laid out in this book step by step. Each phase sequentially builds on each other to help you get consistent traction and momentum.

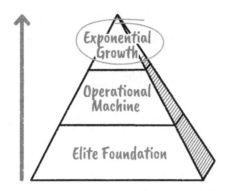

If even one piece is off, you won't get the results you know are possible. And this is exactly why most entrepreneurs are *stuck* and not growing even though they're working hard and trying a lot. By executing the other steps, marketing then becomes so much easier and better. Trust me.

Let me put it this way: In the first 90-day sprint of our 2X Accelerator program, we talk about marketing directly less than 10% of the time. Still, our *average* six-figure client has more than doubled their revenue. That's in just 90 days!

How is this? There is so much value to drive more growth more easily in the other steps as well. It is not about tactics, like most teach.

If you don't have a clear strategy, an irresistible offer, fulfillment and operations not ready to go, you are stuck in the weeds, aren't clear on your numbers, and everything else I've talked about so far, then trying marketing tactics just won't work. You'll be burning a lot of money and time trying to force people to buy from you. That doesn't work!

If you're anything like me, you've hired a few marketing agencies. You join marketing programs or coaches. And they all haven't worked out great, right?

But the thing is…it's not their fault. In fact, most of it is *your* fault.

I know because I hired Facebook Ads agency…after agency…after agency… each with a new promise of easily printing money for me.

However, they all failed miserably. Why?

Mostly because of me. I set them up to fail.

They were marketing:

- *Decent* content (at best)…
- That wasn't hitting their true pains/desires…
- For a product that was *not* differentiated (and definitely not "irresistible") or validated (true product-market fit)…
- With a sales process that wasn't very strategic or proven.

On top of that, I wasn't maximizing customer value (LTV). I wasn't making raving fans. I didn't know the numbers well enough to fix the problems. I wasn't using much social proof. And much more.

In short, I was setting these marketing agencies up to fail!

And that they did. It wasn't their fault. It was mine. As a result, I burned through a lot of hard-earned money and literally years of time thinking that they were going to fix things. When in fact, the path to big growth and success does *not* start with marketing.

The fastest path to where you want to go—with the freedom, the profits, the consistency—is to follow the 2X Formula and the steps in this book, one element at a time.

Trust me, you do need marketing. Just don't skip the other steps or you'll be like other entrepreneurs—running in place on the six-figure hamster wheel. The order matters a lot.

With that being said, I *do* want to show you some marketing strategies that *work* so that you can drive your machine to some incredible growth. Let's get into it.

Where All Your Answers Are

Okay, so you're ready to scale now, right?

You have your business machine in place, more time than ever, improved systems, and a world-class team that is clear and aligned. Now it's time for the next step: marketing.

So where do you begin?

> Facebook ads?
> Social media?
> Videos?
> PR?

Nope! None of the above.

Start with your Ideal Target Audience.

The thing is…

Your ITA has all of the answers!

They are the ones you're serving. They are the ones who pay the bills. Your entire business is built around them.

So stop trying to figure it all out yourself. Stop trying to guess what will work. Stop doing what *you* think you should do.

The million-dollar marketing hack is simply tapping into your audience for the answers. This is so simple that most don't do it, but *you* should. **The more intimately you understand them and are connected with them, the easier and better your solutions will be.**

Once you know who your ideal customer is, go and get the information you need. Here's a few simple ways how:

1 - Surveys

Our 2X clients know that we *love* getting information from them via surveys so that we can give them the best, most customized experience.

What they don't know at the time is that it's such valuable marketing information we need, too!

We ask for surveys:

1. To apply for our 2X Accelerator
2. As the first step once you get accepted
3. At 30 days to check in and gauge where you're at
4. At 90 days to hear about your experience and results
5. At the end of the in-person 2X Mastermind event

We love getting this information.

It tells us their entire journey—from their pains and goals, to why they invested, why now, where they found us, their situation beforehand, their biggest takeaways, the transformation, the revenue growth and results they've achieved, etc.

It's all there! Not only does this help us create a better client experience, fix problems, and make raving fans. It's marketing gold so that we can reverse-engineer what pains and goals we need to address in our marketing. Plus, the stories, challenges, and breakthroughs are endless.

2 - Interview

Another great way to understand your ITA is to do what seems almost crazy to some, and that's actually talk to your ideal audience.

I know, it's a wild concept. Pick up the phone, do a video call, or meet them in person, and just ask them a few questions.

The company who understands their market the best wins.

Ultimately, you want to understand their pains, fears, emotions, and situations so you can better market to your ideal audience. You want to understand what their true day-to-day situation looks like. What do they struggle with, what are the details they have to deal with. The more that you can understand them, the more that you can communicate directly to them in your marketing. This is key.

And then here's another million-dollar marketing hack that seems way too simple:

Use their exact words and phrases in your messaging and copy!

Use their stories and examples. Explain the emotions and details. You'll find this all connects with your audience much more than the bland marketing most companies use.

Your ideal audience has all the answers—including the best copy you could ever have. So use it.

Stop trying to guess and figure it all out. Go to the source and ask them. They can give you the shortcut.

Let's recap the process:

1. Identify who your ideal customers are.
2. Go deep in understanding them through surveys, interviews, and working one-on-one.
3. Learn from them to figure out exactly how and where to market, what to sell, etc.
4. Use their exact words, stories, and examples in your marketing.
5. And continue to repeat this process.

By doing so, not only are you saving yourself from having to figure it all out—your audience will tell you. You'll save time time and energy while you'll see your conversions and connection go through the roof.

The one who wins in any niche is the one who understands their market the best. Now, with this strategy, that is you.

6-Figure Hustler	7-Figure CEO
• Make decisions based on gut and intuition • Creates first and then tests how well it will work after • Has your marketing be about you, not the customer	• Knows that your audience has all of the answers • Regularly gets information and feedback from clients; has a very good pulse on their real-life situation • Uses exact stories, scenarios and client words in your copy to convert • Sets up systematic ways to continue to get feedback

The Five-Word Marketing Strategy

Simplicity. It's one of our superpowers at 2X, and I want it to be one of yours, too.

A key area where almost all six-figure entrepreneurs need to simplify is with your marketing.

You don't need ten marketing channels. You don't need to keep trying tactic after tactic. You don't need every new tech tool.

The gurus out there make you feel like there's some secret marketing 'easy button' where leads just appear overnight. Press it and *boom*, you're rich and famous. They make you feel like you're totally missing out without it. But if you give in, which most do, you often quickly find you're adding more complexity, more costs, more to learn, more tasks, more tech tools, more work for you and your team—but less time and no more profits!

That doesn't sound like the right move.

Luckily, we have a different, simpler, much more profitable approach to marketing. Is it as sexy and shiny as everyone else's? Nope, not so much.

But you know what *is* sexy? *Results*—and you living your dream life, making more money, and having more freedom than ever.

Now *that* is sexy.

So here's our seven-figure marketing strategy summarized down into five powerful words:

Do more of what works.

That's it.

Do more of what works.

Follow this, and you'll be on the fast-track to seven figures and blowing by your competition. Don't be afraid of how simple this is.

Look, you've gotten to six figures—that means something has worked. Well, now it's time to double down and do more of that and **stop doing what doesn't work!** It's not rocket science, but we all overcomplicate it.

Marketing Channels Breakdown

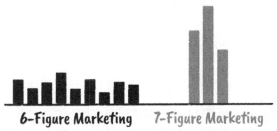

6-Figure Marketing   7-Figure Marketing

You can get to seven figures in revenue with ONE primary marketing channel, one product, and one ITA. We've seen it over and over again.

Keep things simple. Especially in marketing. Some stuff you've been doing works, and most doesn't. So simply cut what doesn't or change your strategy. And for the stuff that does, **do more of it!**

This is exactly what we do with client after client: dive in, see what they've been doing, understand the numbers, cut what doesn't work (which are most things)... and double down on what does.

This simplicity and focus on their top revenue strategy helped James Hodges scale his business from $55,833 per month to $144k in two months after joining 2X, setting the foundation for many millions ahead!

It helped Reuben Driedger of Coaches Creating Impact create an ongoing marketing machine by duplicating his best strategy, scaling from an average of $20,835 to over $55,000 per month in just 90 days and then over six figures _per month_ shortly after that.

Alex Schlinsky, the founder of Prospecting On Demand, also already had a six-figure business coming into 2X, and he tripled his business in 45 days by simply doubling down on what was working well and cutting what didn't!

Know your numbers...

Simplify and cut what doesn't work...

Do more of what does...

And keep repeating this as you scale quickly to seven figures and beyond.

6-Figure Hustler	7-Figure CEO
• Always wants to try new things and do more • Has a lot of marketing channels, none of which are optimized • Running on intuition with no real visibility into the actual metrics that matter	• Is looking more often what to cut and where to simplify instead of what to add • Lives by the five word marketing strategy of 'Do More Of What Works' • Knows the numbers in and out • Understands that one or two truly dialed in marketing channels can generate millions in sales

Tap Into The Goldmine

The fact of the matter is, you're sitting on a goldmine.

There are a lot of sales within reach that you aren't tapping into properly. We see this day-in and day-out with clients across the globe.

Again, we want to keep things simple. So instead of trying to get new leads and running a big, expensive marketing campaign, let's help you maximize your sales and leads by being strategic.

So, after years of proving these out, here are the seven most common levers we use to drive growth—and you should, too!

1 - Raving Fans

Your best customers are your best customers.

Your happiest, most successful clients who love your product/service are the most likely to buy *more* from you in the future. Most forget this and ignore them, leaving a bunch of money (and much deeper relationships with their best customers) on the table.

But your raving fans should get a lot of time and attention because they are your best and most profitable customers. Plus, they're the best ones to see what additional products and services you should offer, bounce ideas off of, and get referrals too. Maximize these relationships!

2 - Current Customers

Then go to the rest of your current customers. There is always a percentage of your customers who want more, better, faster. Give them those options!

Whether it's selling more of the same product, keeping your clients much longer, additional higher-end offerings, or other new services/products you can offer them, make sure you are very strategic about maximizing lifetime value.

Studies show that the likelihood of current customers buying from you in the future is exponentially higher than new leads, so let's make sure we capitalize on these. Again, most entrepreneurs ignore their current customers. Put the systems in place to keep them longer, and keep selling them new products. LTV is the best lever, so use it.

3 - Current Leads In Pipeline

As we discussed in Chapter 6, improving sales conversions is a key lever to scale to the next level.

You likely have a lot of potential business with your current leads, so don't forget to nurture and manage them using some of the sales strategies discussed in Chapter 6 to get your conversions to the next level.

Most businesses we work with want to immediately focus on getting *new* leads, but we always find that there's a good amount of revenue within reach of already interested leads with the right *irresistible* offer and approach. Don't look past this group!

4 - Referrals

Your best form of *new* leads come from referrals.

When someone vouches for you, the leads they generate are pre-sold and some of the best customers you can get. Studies show they are four times more likely to buy, they pay you more, stay with you longer, *and* drive more profits.[6]

The problems are:

- Most entrepreneurs don't have great fulfillment turning regular customers into raving fans who do refer.
- And most never ask for referrals either! They hope and pray they just happen.

---

[6] Duskin, Chris. "15 Referral Marketing Statistics You Need To Know." *Extole*, 31 July 2017, https://www.extole.com/blog/15-referral-marketing-statistics-you-need-to-know/

Instead, turn your business into a self-fulfilling growth machine with best-in-class fulfillment and a strong referral system. If you do, you'll be growing on auto-pilot. We call this 'organic viral loops.'

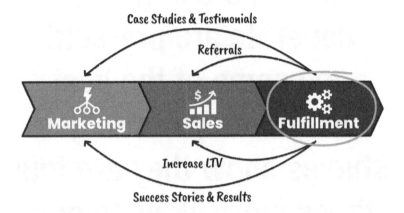

Just imagine if every customer was so happy that they referred one other customer. Your business would be growing on auto-pilot with zero marketing at all! That's the power of raving fans and referrals.

Consider three to seven ways you can ask for referrals throughout your customer's journey. Done right, you'll have a consistent stream of the best leads money can buy and a very strong and healthy business.

5 - Your #1 Marketing Channel

Remember, do more of what works. What we do every time we come into a new company to help them scale, we streamline, systemize and scale the top marketing channel. Usually there is a big opportunity to 2-4x the number of leads that come from a top channel.

Imagine if you took your biggest marketing channel and turned it into a MACHINE.

What do you think would happen? You'd exponentially grow your leads and consistency, right?

So focus on growing and systemizing your current working channels first before adding any new untested strategies.

6 - Past Customers

And don't forget your past customers! This can easily be one of your top revenue and referral sources, but odds are that you don't give enough time or focus here. Do you have good client communication and maximization systems in place? Do you keep in touch with past customers even after they're done buying from you?

This is a gold mine by itself if you tap into it, and it doesn't take much time.

As business legend Keith Cunningham asks, *"How big would your business be if you still had every customer that ever tried you?"*

7 - Past Leads

When's the last time you reached out to past leads? Have you continued to nurture them since they showed interest?

Per a study, 80% of sales are made from the fifth to twelfth contact. That's a lot of sales you may be leaving behind!

If you don't have it already, create a plan of how you can effectively follow up and continue to strengthen your relationship with past leads on auto-pilot. Then, tap into them, and you may be surprised how much business you come up with.

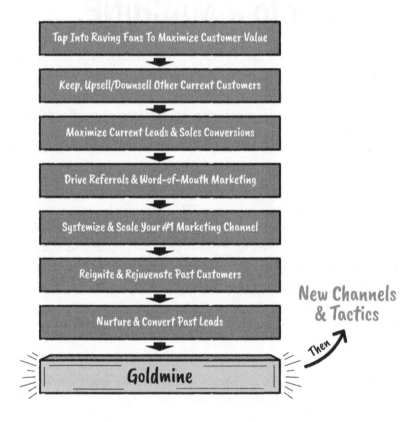

The cool thing is, none of these seven strategies cost you much money. And most are right within reach! They're fast, easier to do, much more profitable, *and* the numbers show they are much more likely to convert.

If you get really strong at each of these, you're going to have a very healthy business.

Give up the addiction and allure of needing new and shiny marketing strategies…and tap into the gold mine underneath your feet.

That's where the real value is.

6-Figure Hustler	7-Figure CEO
• Addicted to getting new leads more than most elements of the business; thinks, *"If I just get more leads, I'll be good."* • Focused on tactics and short-term, not fundamental long-term drivers • Is looking for new instead of maximizing what is within reach • No systems to maximize the true value of customers or leads	• Takes the simplest path to growth • Knows the highest-impact ways to grow revenue and profit (the goldmine) • Approaches growth in a strategic order, maximizing customer value before putting the focus on generating new leads • Creates the strategy and systems to continually maximize each 'goldmine' lever above

Million-Dollar Positioning

In one of my previous businesses, we worked with author-entrepreneurs to help them launch their books into bestseller status and use it as a tool to quickly grow their brand and business.

What I stumbled into in this business is a key to marketing success:

Having the right positioning.

The first thing we'd do is upgrade and optimize the positioning of each author, business, and book (even for those who were elite entrepreneurs or New York Times best-selling authors). Before we started to market anything, we knew we had to get this right. And most of the time, we did.

The result was over 1.7 million books moved (which is a lot!) and millions of dollars earned on the back end for these authors within our first two years in business.

You have only the blink of an eye to capture someone's attention, so positioning is key. To help optimize your positioning and maximize your marketing conversions, we've created a framework called Million Dollar Positioning™ (MDP).

This framework will help you stand out from the crowd, and includes the four main elements below.

1 - Strategic Differentiation

We talked about this in Chapter 2, but it's worth repeating.

You need to understand your competition, and make yourself *different* and better. Different is the key word here. You need to put yourself in a category of one.

You can't be all things to all people, so get specific on your audience, and then choose and leverage your differentiating factors wisely.

The vast majority of six figure businesses are not differentiated much at all. They aren't specific, targeted, or unique. And it makes it nearly impossible to get ahead from a marketing standpoint. So get differentiated and create no competition.

Why should someone do business with you (instead of all of their other options)?

- What can your product/service do that no other product can?
- How do you solve the key pain in a better way than anyone else?

Consider these and make your business stand out.

2 - Own A Phrase

> *"The most powerful concept in marketing is*
> *owning a word in the prospect's mind."*
> —Al Ries and Jack Trout, *The 22 Immutable Laws Of Marketing*

Look at any market leader, and you'll likely see that they own a word or phrase used by their target audience. This isn't a coincidence!

The best marketers strategically craft this to happen.

Owning a phrase helps drive word-of-mouth marketing, improves sales conversions, gets you media features, and much more.

At a previous company of mine, Epic Launch, we wanted to own the phrase 'book launch' for our ITA, and we did for a while. As a result, we had a constant flood of new, qualified, and interested leads—so much that we didn't have to do *any* marketing at all!

No social media. No advertising. We didn't even have an email opt-in or funnel of any kind. We just had a couple pieces of content, had a great service, and became known for the phrase 'book launch,' leading to almost seven figures in sales organically before we started *actually* marketing.

That's the power of owning a phrase.

Now at 2X we are known for the word 'systems' to our audience of business owners. The vast majority of clients that come into the 2X Accelerator program are pre-sold on us and the idea that they need *systems* to make their business much more repeatable and scalable without more hours. That makes us a no-brainer for them.

Now it's your turn.

> *What is the word or phrase you are going to own?*

> *What words or phrases, if you were known for them in your niche, would allow you to get to seven figures and beyond?*

Then start to create a game plan of how you're going to own these.

Identify your ideal positioning, become the go-to for that thing, and your marketing won't look back.

3 - Massive Social Proof

Not many things can sell quite like social proof, and it changes your positioning in a heartbeat.
So follow this process:

1. Create great products.
2. Turn customers into raving fans and big success stories.
3. Have those people share their experiences and thoughts.
4. Share those testimonials strategically and often, which will impact your conversions.
5. Watch your business grow…and repeat!

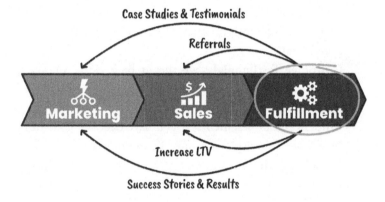

As you can see, this again goes back to great fulfillment driving so much of this. This is a key focus area to scale your business to seven figures and beyond.

And the fact is,

There is no such thing as too much social proof!

So don't hold back. Use it often on your website and in marketing. As it's one thing if you sell your products/services, but a completely different thing if others sell it for you.

Here are the types of social proof you can use to help you have Million Dollar Positioning™:

a. **Public Reviews**: on public channels like Google Maps, Yelp, Facebook, Amazon

b. **Big Media Features**: like on Forbes or big outlets (i.e. top podcasts) in your niche

c. **Social Media Following**: a vanity metric, but having a lot of followers will make some people think you are important regardless

d. **Case Study Features**: featuring a breakdown of before and after, and the transformation; this is more in-depth than just a testimonial

e. **Customer Testimonials**: whether it be a video, quote, social post, or email, you should get a lot of testimonials and leverage them!

f. **Influencer Endorsements**: if you have endorsements from big names in your niche, you must be important, right? Get these and leverage them

g. **Big Name Association**: get associated with the big names that your ITA will recognize

h. **Credibility**: have certifications or degrees, or my favorite—*results*! Share them!

Start with the low-hanging fruit. What from this list can you leverage to upgrade your positioning in the next week? Do those first.

Then have an ongoing system for capturing testimonials and case study features.

Improve each of these eight types of social proof over time, and you will most definitely take a leap in your stance as the market leader.

4 - Authority Content

You don't need a ton of content, but the *right* content is powerful.

Depending on your business, maybe this is a really well-done branded PDF guide (that you can use for email opt-ins), or maybe it's a webinar, whitepaper, book, or simply a few core pillar blog posts.

A collection of content helps for sure, but a few really well-done pieces that position you as the market leader and topic authority for your ITA are way more powerful. We've seen this over and over again.

What are your core pieces of content that if someone would view would make them highly likely to do business with you? Get clear on this and make it great.

If you have a lot of content but aren't gaining traction with it, slow things down and make a few world-class pieces that position you as the authority.

But the key is to strategically craft this overall. Million-dollar marketing begins with Million Dollar Positioning™.

More leads, more exposure, better conversions, and higher prices—this one lever drives so much, so create an action plan to improve each one of these areas ASAP.

6-Figure Hustler	7-Figure CEO
• Afraid to narrow down, so stays broad and general • Doesn't differentiate from the marketplace, and as a result sets marketing and sales up to struggle • Not filling a big gap or need in the marketplace • Not strategically different and better than the alternatives	• Knows a key part of marketing and getting more traction is having the right positioning • Positioning is differentiated, specific, and filling an unmet or underserved need in the marketplace • Own a phrase in the mind of your ITA • Consistently leverage various forms of social proof • Create authority content pieces to leverage and reinforce that market leader position

Marketing's Secret Weapon

In most businesses, big or small, it's not 'sales *and* marketing.' It's closer to 'sales *versus* marketing.'

Marketing says that the sales team isn't closing the leads. The sales team says the leads aren't qualified. Pretty soon they forget that they're on the same team!

Marketing's secret weapon is simple: great sales conversions.

So if you want to scale your marketing, then you better adopt this mentality and get marketing and sales to work closely.

The first major piece to work with your sales on is in crafting an irresistible offer. A truly irresistible offer that we talked about in Chapter 2 will make your sales team look like heroes, and as a result make marketing easy.

So, craft and validate a strategic offer that is too good to pass up. That's where to begin.

Then from there, remember the key that your ITA has *all* the answers. And your sales and fulfillment teams each have incredible intel on them! So tap into them to keep refining and optimizing as you scale.

Your sales team knows who buys and why. They know who doesn't and why. All you need to do, then, is address the problems for why they don't buy in your marketing and double down on why they do.

Voilà! You are a marketing genius. (Even if it's not rocket science.)

Sometimes you feel like you have to be brilliant in your marketing, but the answers are all right within reach. And there is a more strategic way to scale than trying to figure it all out yourself and try every marketing tactic out there.

Get strategic, and trust me, your conversions will go through the roof.

6-Figure Hustler	7-Figure CEO
• Sales team and other departments are often in a silo, not working together • Not a great flow of information from sales (objections, why they buy, etc.) back to marketing to improve marketing	• You work together with sales to make conversions better, setting up marketing to scale knowing that sales is a strength • You know that so much of marketing and sales begins with an irresistible offer, so you work to create that along with the sales team • Good flow of feedback between sales and marketing on what's working, what's not, objections, and more to optimize marketing and get prospects '80% sold' for sales

Growth Or Death

Entrepreneurs are often shocked that their business isn't growing. Then I ask them two simple questions:

- *What are the most impactful marketing and growth activities you can do?*
- *How much time are you spending doing those each day?*

That's when they stumble, insert excuses, and share that not only are they working on the wrong marketing activities, but they **aren't spending enough time marketing at all!**

Your business doesn't grow magically just because you have potential. As CEO, you have to *drive* that growth. This should be your main role as you scale to $1 million and beyond.

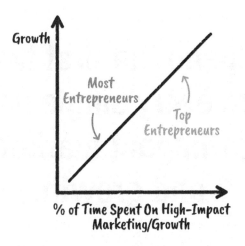

If you aren't putting what's needed for proper marketing—resources, energy, money, focus, team, time—then you won't drive the growth that you're after.

Most get lost on the marketing teeter-totter. They spend time on marketing, get some clients, then have to go into fulfillment or fix fires that pop up. So, they stop marketing…and as a result their lead generation slows down. Then, they have to *scrap and claw* to get some sales.

It's a never-ending roller coaster. We have to put an end to this!

When you look at your time in detail, **a minimum of 60% should be focused on growth.**

By doing so, you're going to set your business up to continually be moving forward. If you combine this with the full team mentality of turning your business into a machine, then you'll not only be driving consistent leads, but you'll be consistently improving each area of your business. That combination is a recipe for some very nice growth!

One simple way to think about it is:

Spend the first two hours every single day on high-impact marketing and growth.

If you do this, your pipeline will always be full. Imagine that! It's easier than you think.

I spent years expecting to have some kind of rocket-ship growth, when in reality, I was only spending ~20% of my time on marketing and growth. Even then, a lot of that marketing was busywork that didn't move the needle, like social media posts.

Do a self-evaluation:

- *What are the most impactful marketing and growth activities you can do?*
- *How much time are you spending doing those each day?*

And how can you exponentially increase your time spent on those high-impact activities?

Set yourself up to win with some simple actions here, and your business will never be the same again.

6-Figure Hustler	7-Figure CEO
• Too stuck in the 'weeds' to drive growth • Time goes in phases; sometimes spending a lot of time on marketing, then having to fulfill or fight fires and take your eye off of marketing • Not clear on the highest impact revenue generating activities	• Spending a minimum of 60% of time on growth • Sets up calendar to always be filling your pipeline for growth • Free from the weeds to work "on" not "in" the business • Clear on the highest impact growth-oriented responsibilities and works to offload everything else

Chapter 7 Big Ideas

- There is a very strategic order to drive consistent, long-term growth and marketing is the last major step to focus on as you scale from six to multiple seven-figures.
    - o By going out of order, you set your marketing up to fail and will lack the conversions that are possible, making things way harder than they need to be.
    - o This is why most six figure businesses get stuck and never get much traction (and why only 4% break through!); it's not from potential, it's from the right strategy and order of attack.
- Know that your audience has all of the answers: ask them, leverage them, and use their stories and phrases in your marketing to really connect with your potential customers.
- Keep marketing simple with the highest impact channels for your specific ITA; one or two truly dialed in marketing channels can generate millions in sales. Get your top channels to full machine status.
- Know your numbers and live by the five word marketing strategy of *Do More Of What Works*.
- Approach growth in a strategic order, maximizing customer value (the goldmine) before trying to generate new leads (the most expensive thing).
- The top levers to optimize for more revenue are:
    - o Raving Fans
    - o Current Customers
    - o Current Leads In Pipeline
    - o Referrals
    - o Your #1 Marketing Channel
    - o Past Customers
    - o Past Leads
- Create the strategy and systems to maximize each element of the seven 'gold mine' levers ongoing, and you'll have an incredibly healthy business.

- So much of your marketing and sales success comes from getting your Million Dollar Positioning™ dialed in. The elements of this are:
  - o Strategic differentiation: creating a category of one
  - o Own a phrase: defining your place in the marketplace and owning it
  - o Massive social proof: leveraging various forms to have others indirectly sell for you
  - o Authority content: establishing and reinforcing your market leader position with strategic assets to give value
- Work strategically with sales to have a good flow of communication back and forth to generate more of the *ideal* leads, that are pre-sold with their top objections already addressed.
- Get clear on the highest impact revenue-generating activities and work daily on these, consistently filling the pipeline with lead and sales so that you escape the up-and-down roller coaster of sales.
- Spend over 60% of time on growth activities, not stuck in the weeds or fighting fires.

CHAPTER 8

MAKING 7-FIGURES YOUR NEW REALITY

"Ideas are easy.
Execution is
everything."
—John Doerr

Let's recap what we've talked about so far, as everything has brought you to this point. Now, it's time to do something about it.

Many entrepreneurs dream of having a seven-figure business that drives a big income, great lifestyle, and lots of freedom, fun, and impact.

But few ever get there.

Why is that?

It's not an issue of talent, resources, desire, or even skill. It's often a matter of execution.

Execution is everything.

And it's now the biggest challenge you face. All of the ideas, actions, and growth strategies you've learned from this book don't matter at all if you don't execute.

This book is laid out in a very specific and strategic order to help make it as easy as possible. Every step builds sequentially on the next to maximize your results without business feeling so damn hard all of the time (*finally!*).

To get maximum traction, it's critical to go deep into each phase one by one. Let's recap the key elements of each step:

Step 1 - It all starts with your mindset and vision. If you don't have the proper state of mind, a) you won't think big and see what's possible, and b) you'll sabotage your success (unconsciously) or take the slow grind there. Everything begins with these two elements.

Your vision drives every business decision.

What do you really want? What does your ideal lifestyle look like?

From there we can get clear on exactly what your strategy, model, team, and everything else needs to look like to help you get *there*. And the clearer you are, the faster you can go, so start here.

Step 2 - Once you're clear on the vision, it's all about building the strategy and model to get you there ASAP. The way we do that is with our Model ONE™ framework. This is arguably the most important step for six figure businesses to nail, and something that you'll want to spend a lot of time on.

The more clear, targeted, simple, and strategic that each element of this formula is, the more that you'll be set up to get traction and momentum across the board. So work through each step here in detail.

Step 3 - Then, it's a matter of getting you free.

The tipping point of business is when you get free from the weeds.

As soon as you do, everything changes.

So take back control of your time and calendar. Fire yourself, delegate, systemize, and empower your team...so that you can be a true CEO working "on" the business. With the proper time, you can achieve anything. So follow this chapter to free up 20+ hours per week.

Step 4 - From here, it's a matter of turning your business into an operational machine. This is the key to lasting consistency, predictability, freedom, cash flow, and growth. Yet few businesses put the proper focus here!

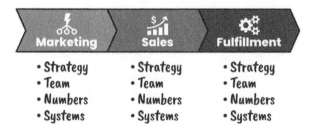

If you do this and combine it with the right strategy and model, you'll be set up for big success for a long time to come. Learn to love systems, the numbers, and great operations and build a culture around these things. You'll be happy that you did.

Step 5 - One of the oldest and best forms of leverage to nail is having the right team around you. The challenge is, this isn't always easy. So, follow the steps in this chapter to get the right people on your team with clarity on what matters and set them up to win.

If you get this right, your entire life will be different. Take it seriously with a few key shifts we discussed.

Step 6 - Then, you're ready to scale. And one of the key levers to do just that is with great, consistent sales conversions.

Most businesses are weak here, relying on pure talent instead of a scalable sales process. But we need to get you free from sales with a repeatable system that maximizes conversions. This will make your marketing numbers look much better and is a huge lynchpin in your business.

Step 7 - And from here, it's about generating more consistent qualified leads to fuel your entire business machine as you grow exponentially. But don't start here. Keep things simple and strategic, building a marketing *machine* as you go.

Done right, by following this order, you get the most out of your time and effort.

You'll then:

- Be hyper clear on where you want to go
- Leading to much easier and better decision making
- With a strategic, simple, strategy and model that is set to scale
- Where you are differentiated and getting more conversions than ever
- As you have the time to work "on" the business, not "in" it (and live your dream life)
- While your business produces consistent results and raving fans
- And you scale exponentially quarter after quarter

This isn't a fantasy. This is your opportunity if you follow the Formula.

The choice is yours.

To wrap things up and get you on the path to seven figures, I want to share a few final strategies to put this stuff into actual practice and help you join the 4%.

None of it is rocket science. You can do it all. And my hope is that you *will* do it all, as we've seen over and over, insane growth and success is possible in a hurry if you follow the steps in this book.

The Momentum Train

Not to overstate things, but an important realization is:

Every decision matters.

Every decision has a ripple effect—often much bigger than you think.

In my first business (which was in day-trading stocks), I got obsessed with the compound effect and how seemingly small actions stacked on top of each other led to some incredible things. It's *the most powerful force in the universe,* per Albert Einstein.

And the compound effect either works *for you* as you build momentum, or *against you* in a downward spiral. This is true for your finances, but even more importantly for your decision-making in business.

Let me share two examples to highlight how this works.

The Compound Effect Working Against You

Let's say you're busy stuck in the 'weeds' of the business. You want to take on a new big client to add more revenue to your business.

But you don't have someone on your team to help do it. You're already redlining, working as hard as you can without burning out, but you need the cash flow so you decide to hire someone.

Since you're in a rush and need the help fast, you don't follow what we've talked about in this book, and you skip past a few steps to quickly hire someone you *think* will be a good fit.

You don't set them up to succeed, expecting them to 'just get it' since it's pretty simple stuff to you. But unfortunately, all that experience you thought they had wasn't really related, and they don't pick things up and contribute.

They cost you time, energy, and hard-earned money. Plus, you realize it would have just been easier to do it yourself. So you do. And back even deeper in the weeds you go…

But now you're behind and even more frustrated and over-whelmed. The client is unhappy, scope creep kicks in and the project grows legs, and, next thing you know, this dream deal a few weeks ago is now a nightmare loss that you can't wait to get past.

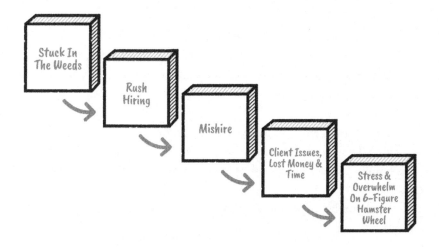

This example is the negative side of the compound effect—seemingly small things that stack up against you. Unfortunately, this is the reality for most hustling entrepreneurs.

The result is you're **working hard, going nowhere fast**—stuck on the never-ending hamster wheel.

Sound familiar? I've been there more often than I'd like to admit.

But the good news is, this all could be avoided. You've had those times when you felt *unstoppable*. Let's look at the impact of the right decisions and how it all builds up to help you get more of that. We call this:

The Momentum Train

> Let's say you follow the steps in this book and get super clear on your vision. From that, you see a few things that are not essential that you can cut out right away. Plus, you get free from the weeds by implementing systems, simplifying your business model, and gain an extra 15 to 20 hours per week total.

> Now you have the time and energy to help optimize your current team, giving them the role clarity, feedback, and key systems to support them. As a result, they quickly start getting more accomplished and are handling more than ever.

> With this, you realize you don't even need to hire someone when that project comes up!

> The project gets executed well and is profitable, and all without you! The client is happy, you stay out of the weeds, you save employee costs, and you're ready for even more.

> Plus, the happy client sends a referral. And *boom*! Things are taking off.

You feel like you have a real business now—one that can run and grow without you having to be involved in everything. As a result, you have the energy, confidence, and infrastructure to do it a lot more. So you do!

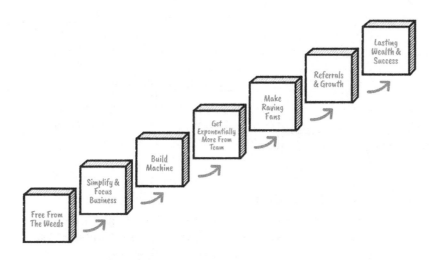

This is the **Momentum Train**.

This is where you have the power, clarity, and some damn *fun* in your business!

This is where **you realize this whole entrepreneurship thing *is* in fact more than worth it**, energizing you and your team more than ever.

This is where you want to be.

And using these 2X principles and this book as your guide, it's where you *will* be. Trust me.

Do you see the difference between both sides—the negative spiral and the positive Momentum Train?

It all started back at the root cause, with a couple of the seemingly small first steps we started this book with—simplifying your business and freeing up your time.

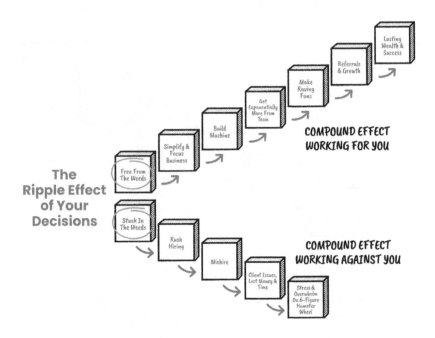

That's why the *order* matters so much— it makes everything else exponentially easier *or* harder.

You choose.

So start small. Step back from the blur of the day-to-day. Take the *right* steps that you know you should, and watch it impact you and your business more than you could ever imagine.

You're only a few tweaks away from a new, more exciting, and more profitable reality. So let's make it happen.

Where To Start

We've talked about a lot.

From who you need to hire and when…to your highest-leverage marketing actions…to the meetings and operations to have in place to scale, and more.

It's a lot to digest, but let's simplify things down to the 80/20 of where to start. Here are the first few steps to get you in motion and onto that Momentum Train.

Step 1 - The Vision

Get clear on the hardest part of all: what you *really* want, and what you want to create in this world with your business.

And never forget:

Your business is a *tool* to create your dream life.

It's not who you *are*. It's not what you *do*.

It is a *vehicle* that can create the:

- Wealth
- Impact
- Freedom

- Experiences
- Growth and momentum
- And whatever else you want in your life!

It is a *tool* to give you the *freedom* to do what you want, when you want, and with the people you want.

Unfortunately, most entrepreneurs create something that gives them the exact opposite: a stressful self-employed job they are tied to with a lot of responsibilities and little (if any) wealth.

Don't be like most entrepreneurs! **Start by getting hyper clear on your vision.** Then design your business intentionally *and* strategically so it will support your dream life.

That's where it all begins.

Take some time, get out of your normal day-to-day, and craft that vision for yourself and your business that inspires you to get moving!

Step 2 - The Reality

Then, figure out where you are now. Go deep into the key numbers and take a good hard look.

> *What's working? What's not?*
> *How is your business really doing?*
> *What are the true root causes holding you back?*
> *Where is the bottleneck? How is each department really doing?*
> *What is your real profitability?*

Take the time to think. Get brutally honest with yourself.

The more you understand reality, the more easily we can fix your issues and unlock big growth. But not before then.

So take the time to reflect and get real.

Most six-figure entrepreneurs avoid this like the plague, defaulting to getting busy and start working. The most successful entrepreneurs however know that…

The fastest path forward is to stop and THINK.

Clarity is power. So get real, get clear, and let's get focused on a strategic path to have you unleash past seven figures (and beyond).

Step 3 - Fast-Action Plan

One very important key to a great day/week/month/year is to *start fast*.

There are surely a lot of ideas you have for what you can do to scale your business. So what are a few quick wins that you can execute in the next 48 hours to start to apply what you've learned?

What are some low-hanging fruit actions? And what are your top three priorities over the next thirty days to go deeper into?

Put a very simple 1-page action plan together, and get into motion right away while this is fresh in your mind. You'll feel the effects in no time.

Step 4 - Nail Your Model ONE™

For every business that we work with, we see a huge opportunity to get more traction more easily by fixing and improving their Model ONE™ strategy substantially. Your business is the same.

Even one element off can make your business so much more difficult to scale!

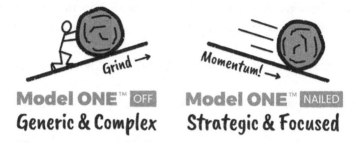

Model ONE™ OFF
Generic & Complex

Model ONE™ NAILED
Strategic & Focused

Get more targeted and strategic. Get more intentional with your offers. Make them irresistible. Set your business up to win and take over your market by nailing this.

I highly recommend you go back to the 7-Figure Strategy chapter and spend a good amount of time here. It can be scary to make these tweaks, but it's truly game-changing when you do. This is the 80/20 of growth.

Your Decision

In my first online business, I interviewed nearly one hundred successful entrepreneurs and investors to pick their brain on what made them wealthy. I was interested in the key turning points that led them on the path to big success.

It was pretty wild to find the commonalities in their stories. No matter what background they had or where they were at in their career, they could clearly articulate a turning point where they made **a decision**.

They saw a better future and decided to go after it. They committed.

And now, it's your turn to make that same decision for yourself.

With this book, you've seen a proven blueprint to take your business (and life) to the next level.

Now it's up to you. You have to *decide*. You have to *commit* to take action and do something about your situation. You have to *choose* to make a few changes, even when it's uncomfortable—because there *will* be times where it's uncomfortable!

My goal is to have you use this book as your launch pad, where you create a business that works *for you*. Where you start growing and making the impact you know is possible. Where you start generating the cash flow and wealth you want. Where you ultimately create the life and business of your dreams.

It's all possible. And it's all within reach.

You just have to make that decision and drive this as a reality for yourself. I can't choose that for you, nor can anyone else.

The *easy* decision, however, is to keep doing what got you to where you are. The hard decision is to take a step back and make some shifts. Remember: what got you here won't get you *there*—to that next level of growth and success.

So, do you truly want to make your vision a reality? Do you want to join the 4% who scale to seven figures and beyond?

Then I challenge you to step up.

Use this book and these resources as your guide. Become that seven-figure CEO right now, starting today, and do what few do: actually apply what you've learned! It's crazy what's possible if you do.

The ripple effect these strategies can make on your family, wealth, mindset, team, clients, and *life* are truly incredible. We see it day in and day out with entrepreneurs all across the world, and I hope to see that in you, as well.

So step up. Be that seven-figure CEO...And turn your business into a consistent, predictable, fast-growing machine.

Your future self will thank you for it.

To your success,
Austin Netzley

THE 7-FIGURE TOOLKIT

Remember: To achieve big success, it's not about ideas or information. It's about implementation and execution.

To help, I have shared a lot of proven strategies and systems that we use ourselves and with our private clients at 2X in a free toolkit of resources including:

- Specific templates
- Example spreadsheets
- Custom PDF worksheets to fill in
- Deep-dive training videos
- And more

This is 100% FREE to access and will help you implement the key strategies and systems into your business. You can access these tools all in one place here:

>> 2X.co/toolkit <<

ABOUT AUSTIN NETZLEY

Austin Netzley is an author, investor, and business growth advisor.

He is the founder and CEO of 2X, a company specializing in helping six- and seven-figure entrepreneurs implement the systems and strategies needed to get free from the day-to-day operations, turn their business into a machine, and start growing faster than ever.

In less than three years, 2X has helped clients generate over $255 million and counting while in the 2X coaching programs.

Austin is a former collegiate athlete and best-selling author who has been featured on many of the world's largest business websites, such as *Forbes*, *Entrepreneur*, *Inc.*, Yahoo!, Business Insider, ABC, NBC, *The Washington Post*, and more.

For more information about Austin and 2X, please visit: 2X.co

ABOUT THE 2X ACCELERATOR

Imagine if your business was a consistent, predictable machine that could run and thrive *without* you. That's what we help you do in the 2X Accelerator.

We work hands-on with ambitious six- and seven-figure online and service-based entrepreneurs to help you implement the proven systems and strategies to take your business and freedom to the next level. We take a holistic approach to business growth, and guide you each step of the way to have your business be a machine.

In just three years, we've helped businesses generate over $255 million while still in our 2X programs…let alone the growth they achieve after 2X.

To learn more about how we can help you break through to the next level, visit:

2X.co/2X
Turn Your Business Into A Consistent,
Predictable, Fast-Growing Machine!

ACKNOWLEDGEMENTS

One of the most important things in life are the people you have around you. I have been blessed in this area my entire life, especially right now!

There are too many people to list here that I'm forever grateful for. But this book would have not been possible without the help and support of the following people:

My Family—For always being there, helping me from when I was a little boy until now, and making me the person I am. I am lucky to have the most amazing family.

My Mentors—From my coaches growing up to the corporate world, the people that got me started in business and those I've never met, thank you.

Our 2X Clients—I strongly believe we have the best client base in the world; you make it fun to do what we do and go the extra mile to support you.

And last but not least…

The 2X Team—It is my mission to build a truly world-class team across the world to help entrepreneurs tap into their potential and grow, and that's what we've done. Across the board, we have a truly special team. There is nobody I'd rather be on this journey with. I appreciate your efforts and work more than you know. You are changing a lot of lives, and the fun is only beginning. Thank you.

ONE LAST THING

Did you enjoy this book?

My hope is that you did. I firmly believe there is a better, simpler, more strategic way to run and grow your business. And this book shares some of the key lessons to do that.

If you did enjoy the book, I'd love to ask you for a favor. **Please share this with at least one entrepreneur who you think could benefit** from these principles and strategies.

Our mission is to help double the number of businesses that scale to seven figures, and that is no easy feat. So, let's change the world...together. Your support makes a huge difference in making that happen.

And lastly, please keep me posted on your progress and success. I would love to hear from you anytime about your progress and make sure that you join the 4%. Reach out anytime by emailing me at <u>austin@2x.co</u>.

I look forward to hearing from you!

Made in United States
North Haven, CT
24 April 2024

51703464R00182